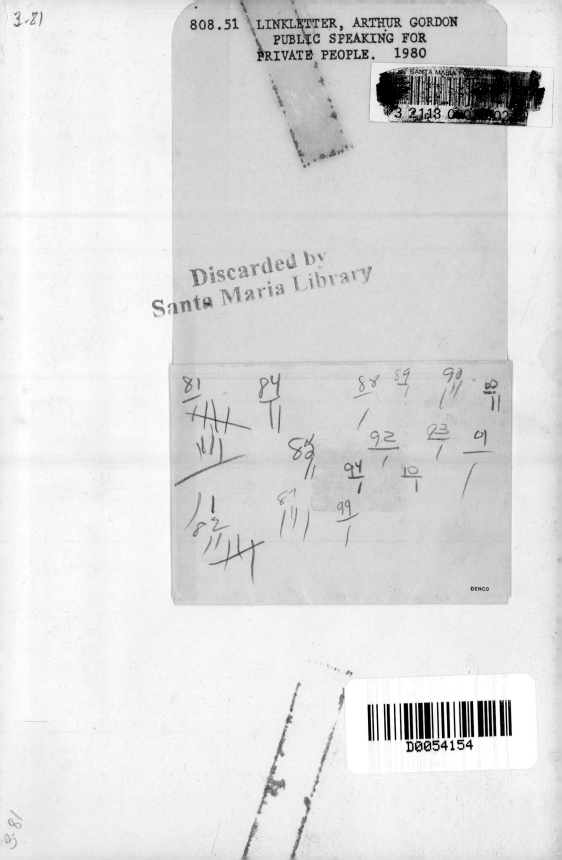

Public Speaking
for Private People

Public Speaking for Private People

by

ART LINKLETTER

❦ ❦ ❦

THE BOBBS-MERRILL COMPANY, INC.
Indianapolis/New York

808.51

Library of Congress Cataloging in Publication Data

Linkletter, Arthur Gordon, 1912-
  Public speaking for private people.

  1. Public speaking.   I. Title.
PN4121.L47   808.5'1   80-691
ISBN 0-672-52652-2

Designed by Jacques Chazaud
Manufactured in the United States of America

First Printing

With deep appreciation
I want to acknowledge
the superb, creative editorial skills
of my friend
William Proctor.

CONTENTS

PART I

❧ ❧ ❧

How to Find
Your Personal
Speaking
Style

CHAPTER ONE

❦ ❦ ❦

A Public Style
for Every
Private Person

I t surprised many people to read in the best-selling *Book of Lists* that man's chief fear in life is getting up to speak in public. This dire dread rates above death, disease, bankruptcy, and an extra month's extension of a mother-in-law's visit.

But I wasn't surprised at all. During the past four decades I've appeared in almost every imaginable speaking situation—from small business meetings, to positive-thinking rallies with twenty thousand people present, to radio and TV shows with audiences that number in the millions. Thousands of other speakers have crossed my path at these events, and no matter how well they may have developed their oral skills, the majority have confessed that at some point they have experienced one common sensation: sheer terror at the thought of standing up before an audience.

Instead of dealing directly with the roots of this fear, many books and speech classes approach the subject with an eye to making polished professional speakers of people. The mistake here is that the average person is *not* going to be a highly experienced public speaker, nor does he *need* to be a public speaker, except occasionally. So my book is intended as a "first-aid kit" directed at those private people who get called on once or twice a year—or once or twice a *decade*—to stand up before a club, a Sunday school class, a school reunion, or the neighborhood coffee klatch to "make a few remarks." My goal is to remove the fear of public speaking from being the average person's Personal Enemy Number One and possibly lower it on the list of human phobias to a position just below leprosy or the black plague.

The first thing to realize is that if you're afraid of speaking before an audience, you're not alone! Some of the greatest public speakers of our day started out as extremely shy, private people whose main strength was that they refused to accept their public inadequacies. For example, take the great preacher and positive-thinking orator Norman Vincent Peale. You'd surely think he was a natural public speaker from childhood, wouldn't you? But listen to this description he gave me of his early years:

"There was a time when I couldn't utter a word in public. As a small boy, I was afflicted with a horrendous inferiority complex. I was shy, reticent, bashful. Now, that word 'bashful' is an old-fashioned word that isn't used much currently. But it's a very descriptive word in that it means to be abashed—and that is exactly what I was!

4

"I was afraid of people. When I would come into a room where my mother had two or three ladies in for an afternoon conversation, I'd be tongue-tied, red in the face, hot and cold all over. I would make a fool of myself, and they would write me off as a shy boy."

The more Norman found himself in public speaking situations, the worse his opinion of himself became. "I just couldn't come through, and I went around telling myself I was a worm, a scared rabbit that didn't amount to anything. Pretty soon, I became aware of the fact that people were agreeing with me. People will usually accept you at your own unconscious self-appraisal."

Finally, this shyness in public led to a personal spiritual crisis while Norman was in college. "I was a sophomore, and a professor took me to task. He was a friend of mine, but he didn't act very friendly that day. He said, 'Norman, when I call on you in class, you get all fouled up. You seem self-conscious, but really, when you're self-conscious, you're *egotistical* because you're thinking about yourself. Why don't you *act like a man for just once in your life*?' "

Norman got very angry and "went out vowing I was going to clean him up! But I didn't do it because he was six feet tall and weighed 250 pounds, so I figured violence wasn't appropriate. And I knew he was right—dead right.

"Well, then, I had a supreme experience. Now everybody ought to have some great experience in his life. I had one that day just after I went out of that professor's office. I walked down and stood on the fourth step from the bottom. I remember exactly where I stood because the experience was so acute. I was always brought up as a Christian—my father was a minister. But that day I said, 'Dear Lord Jesus Christ, please help me! I don't want to be this way anymore! You changed over drunks and thieves

5

and harlots and those people—can't you change me? Can't you take away this terrible inferiority feeling?' "

After this prayer, Norman recalls, he felt "a strange sense of quiet. I heard no voice, felt no hand, nothing like that. I just felt very quiet and confident. And then I began to feel very happy and released. I believe in instant changes in people because I had an instant change."

The next day, he got some reinforcement for this experience from another professor, who wasn't even aware of Norman's conversation with the first man. This second professor suggested that Norman might find help for his speaking problem by delving into the writings of Emerson, Thoreau, Marcus Aurelius, and William James.

"I got interested and fascinated by those people because they talked about what you could do with the human mind," Norman remembers. "Especially William James, the father of American psychological science, who said, 'the greatest discovery in my generation is that a human being can alter his life by altering his attitudes of mind.' "

From this point on, Norman Vincent Peale embarked on a lifelong process of becoming one of the most inspiring speakers of our generation. With his characteristic modesty he cautioned me, "I don't consider myself much of a public speaker." But don't you believe it! I've seen him weave an almost magical spell around huge crowds. And I also know he has developed the very special capacity to strengthen the meager inner resources of those who are suffering from inferiority complexes like his.

On one occasion, for example, he attended a Chicago Rotary Club where a man was delivering an address. Norman noted that the fellow, who was not an expert, was doing a good job getting his message across.

Norman walked over to the speaker after he had finished and said, "I enjoyed your talk very much."

"You're the one who got me up here," the man replied.

Somewhat disconcerted, Norman asked, "How did I get you up here?"

"I had this terrible fear, the greatest fear in my life, of standing up before people," he said. "But then I read one of your books in which you quoted Emerson—that the only way to conquer fear is to *do* the thing that you fear. So I decided to start making talks—at first in Sunday school class, then my farmers' meetings, and finally I've hit the top, here in Chicago at the Rotary Club. The only reason I'm doing this is that I'm sick of being afraid to do it."

"Boy, you really do know how to take yourself in hand," Norman said—and I'd have to agree with that assessment one hundred percent.

But what about you? Do you know how to take *yourself* in hand when you step up to speak before a strange group? Chances are, if you're like most people, you get sweaty palms, a nervous stomach, and an almost overwhelming urge to run in the opposite direction while you're waiting to be introduced to address a group of a dozen or more people.

But the outlook for your becoming a decent speaker, one who can actually feel *comfortable* before an audience, is rather bright if you'll just follow a few simple procedures I've found to be helpful in my own experience. Before we get started, though, let me point out three basic weaknesses that practically everybody suffers from and that you'll learn to master as you develop an effective public style.

7

Weakness 1:
Lack of Self-Confidence.

As Norman Vincent Peale has indicated, good public speaking usually can be traced back to a healthy sense of self-confidence. And self-confidence is either something you're born with or something your parents inculcate in you at an early age—or it's something you have to set out aggressively to acquire. Dr. Peale's route to self-confidence—being able to accept yourself because you realize that God accepts you—is a classic approach too.

But I also think that at the root of this lack of self-confidence you'll often find an almost debilitating fear of failure. From childhood, we've been cautioned, "Don't make a fool of yourself!" Or, "Don't embarrass us with silly remarks." Or, "Be quiet so people won't think you're an idiot." Or, "Never be a show-off!"

Such remarks will put a damper on almost any child's natural enthusiasm. And even more important for our purposes, at an early age many kids become reluctant to stand up and speak their minds in groups. They're afraid of making a mistake or looking silly because they've been *taught* to be afraid. As a result, they're well on their way to a serious erosion of self-confidence.

Weakness 2:
Lack of Practice.

Most of us get little opportunity to speak in public, except for the traditional line or two of dialogue in a church play or school recital. When you were called on in school, you may have floundered around like Norman Vincent Peale did. Or at best, you may have responded with a terse factual answer to a question about history or arithmetic, but with very little time to get involved in a free flow of oral argument and persuasion before your classmates. To overcome this deficiency, it's important to create opportunities for speaking practice, and I'll spend some time showing you exactly how to do this with a minimum of mental pain and discomfort.

A lack of speaking practice may not only be the result of a lack of opportunity, though. Many people actively avoid opportunities to stretch their vocal cords before others. They lack the *will* to seek out arenas to improve their skills, so they in effect cut themselves off from developing an effective personal style of public speaking. I want to work on this underlying volitional problem that may be keeping you from practicing your verbal abilities before others. If you stick with me over the following pages, there's a good chance you'll be able to say, as Norman Vincent Peale did, "I had a high degree of an emotional jolt that *rocked* me. I'd come to the point where I *wanted* to be changed, where I *wasn't willing* to settle for being that way anymore."

That's what I want for you. I want to help you undergo an inner transformation that will enable you to *want* to communicate the important things I know you have to say. I've rarely met a truly uninteresting, boring person. Everybody has something to say that's worth hearing, and it's a tragedy that most people don't know how to say it. Some have talked themselves into thinking they're boring. Or they've acquired a veneer, an outer shell of boredom because they've slipped unwittingly into an uninteresting style of expressing themselves. What I want to do is show you how, if you're simply willing to try to improve your speaking style and engage in a few enjoyable exercises with your family and friends, you can be well on your way—almost overnight—to becoming a passably good speaker.

Weakness 3:
A Tendency to Focus on Your Forensic Flaws Rather Than Your Strengths.

Very few people take naturally to all kinds of public speaking. Usually a person has one or two natural strengths in public speaking. But, ironically, more often than not he fails to capitalize on those strengths.

One of the best illustrations of this weakness that I've encountered personally was a problem faced by former President Richard Nixon. Nixon is an example of a person who made himself over from a very private person into a public person by sheer willpower, guts, determination, and brains. As a young man he was quiet and introverted—a real nontalker, or "Silent Sam." But while he was in college he decided he wanted to be a lawyer, a professional who would be required to speak in public, so he carefully fashioned himself into a speaker.

What was missing, though, was that he was not a natural platform orator. He lacked an outgoing, expansive, dramatic personality; and this flaw always showed up as he made public appearances. As he grew older, he did get better and better by forcing himself to make more speeches, but he was constantly criticized for lacking warmth. His speeches just didn't sound as sincere as they should have sounded.

I became friendly with him as his political career was in its ascendancy. One day, while we were flying from San Francisco to Los Angeles just before his election to his first term as President, I asked, "Are you going to run for the Presidency?"

"Yes, I am," he replied.

"Well, let me give you some professional advice," I said. "Make as few speeches as you can. You *have* to make

10

some, of course, in places where there will be large audiences and microphones. But that's where you're at your weakest. Your greatest strength, on the other hand, is in conversations with just a few people. Fortunately for you, this intimate, conversational approach comes across best on television—and TV is the greatest, most powerful communicating and selling medium we have. As a matter of fact, TV is absolutely perfect to enable you to sit around with just a few people popping questions at you and you answering them. Also, you're really better off talking without any papers or notes. The best TV talk is spontaneous conversation, and you're a conversational whiz. But I've noticed that the more people who are added to an audience, the more stilted you get."

I also told him that when he *had* to make a regular speech to a large crowd, he should speak as informally as he could, preferably without notes. He was a better talker than a speaker, and what he might sacrifice in organization with a prepared speech, he would more than make up for in spontaneity and warmth if he talked off-the-cuff. Like most people, he wasn't an actor, and he couldn't pull off dramatic gestures and flourishes in the same way a natural speaker like John Connally can. Nixon was stiff in front of a big group, and he got even stiffer when he tried to read from a prepared text or memorize a set speech. But he could charm the pants off you if you were the only one in the room with him. It was this strength I encouraged him to exploit in his campaign, and he did take my advice, as he acknowledged later on a number of occasions. I think the result was a more effective campaign for the Presidency. The Watergate fiasco has largely obscured just how popular he was and how well he came across in his public appearances in 1968 and 1972.

So I believe there are natural limitations in trying to

turn yourself into a certain type of speaker. You can learn to make fairly lively openings, organize your thoughts more clearly, and speak with a minimum of audible pauses. But each of us is naturally stronger in some phase of public communication than in others. The secret to a successful public style is to find your strengths and use them to the hilt, as Nixon did, rather than unconsciously slip into areas in which you're weak.

This is just another way of saying you should stick as close to your own personality as you can when you stand up before a group. If you're naturally a quiet, reserved person, you shouldn't try to turn into a dramatic, florid orator when you step onto a platform. And if you *do* try this Dr. Jeckyl–Mr. Hyde routine, at the worst you'll thoroughly embarrass yourself, and at the best you'll probably come across as an insincere, cardboard character.

I don't want to dwell on your weaknesses anymore at this point. I just want you to confront them head-on at the outset and recognize that, even though they're there, you can overcome them. Practically everybody starts out with a frightened feeling of inadequacy, but I can assure you that there's more than mere hope for you. There's a good chance that, with the proper approach, you can emerge from your private little shell and actually build a reputation as a welcome—and perhaps even fascinating—public communicator.

Now, let's start your journey from private to public person at square one: learning to speak more effectively without having to deliver an actual speech.

CHAPTER TWO

♔ ♔ ♔

Secret Speeches

T he major reason people are afraid of public speaking is that they're afraid of the public. So let's begin your journey toward effective speaking by leaving out the "public" for the time being.

There are several ways to go about this. First, go into your bathroom, take off your clothes, and step into a nice hot shower. With the water going full blast, open your mouth and say in a normal tone of voice, "Good evening, folks!"

Ridiculous? Not at all. One of your main problems as a speaker is that you don't speak enough. The more you speak out loud *as though you are speaking in public* (even if the

13

"public" isn't present), the better you'll get. While you're standing there in the shower, you're about as protected from the public as you can be—unless you drive out into the middle of some remote wilderness. In case somebody should happen to hear a garbled sound or two over the roar of the water, he'll just assume you're singing or muttering in the shower the way every normal person does. It's a completely no-threat situation!

Next, while you're still standing in the shower, imagine there are some people before you and try a few "silly" sentences. You might say, "Good evening, folks. . . . Unaccustomed as I am to speaking about world affairs while naked as a jaybird—I like it!" Complete nonsense, but very important as a first step in your effort to turn yourself into a good public speaker. The main idea behind this exercise is twofold: (1) to get you into the habit of seeing yourself in the *attitude* and *posture* of a public speaker, and (2) to give you practice in hearing yourself speak out loud before an audience, even if the audience is imaginary.

Warning: Do *not* imagine you're addressing an audience of thousands. If you do, chances are you'll freeze and you may even experience an anxiety attack. I don't want to turn you off even before we really get started! So limit that shower "audience" to just a few people, maybe a dozen or so old friends. After all, how many people can you crowd into one shower!

Now, try the exercise again in a slightly louder voice—but this time step outside the shower and watch yourself in the bathroom mirror as you speak. Keep loose and natural, and remember: What you say doesn't have to make a bit of sense. The running water is covering the sound, so just keep it coming, one complete sentence after the other on any topics that pop into your head. It doesn't matter, by the way, if you have to stop for a few moments

14

as you wait for a thought to come to mind. Pauses are a key part of any good speech, so the sooner you get used to silent spaces in your delivery, the better.

But perhaps I'm going too fast for you. Some people find they have to take an intermediate step before they go any further. Some may freeze at the sight of themselves in a mirror. Others quail at the thought of imagining any audience, no matter how few people are in it. To get more comfortable, you might try moving from the shower to a closet or to a deserted room in the house and repeat the same exercise. If you're having an extremely difficult time thinking of anything to say, no matter how nonsensical, just repeat your name a few times. Then say the names of your family members and closest friends. Next, try saying a few things about yourself and then about each person you've named. For example: "My name is Susan Smith, and I'm determined to become a good public speaker. My mother's name is Maud Smith, and she is an excellent cook. . . ."

As you try these simple exercises in different locations, you'll quickly catch up with the rest of us, who are still babbling in front of our bathroom mirrors!

After you've spent a few days speaking out loud to your mirror, under the cover of the shower water, you'll be ready to move out of your bathroom and into the world. But don't worry! You're not going to appear before a real audience yet. You're still in the "secret" stage of your speech making, so nobody has to know what you're about.

At this point, though, I do want to put you in contact with a real person. Start with your family or a very close friend. You're not ready yet for practice in front of outsiders, no matter how much confidence your shower-speaking experience has given you. Effective public speaking is a step-by-step experience, with the first steps being as short and measured as possible. If you try to move ahead too quickly, you may fall flat on your face, lose whatever confidence you have gained, and be discouraged from continuing with the program at all. So keep these first speeches simple, short, and "silent," in the sense that nobody but you and I are to know what you're doing.

This silence or secrecy about your objective is especially important as you venture out to your initial encounter with a real person because if you should mention what you're doing to your relative or friend, there is always the chance that, no matter how understanding he is, he may laugh or even sneer at your approach. You don't need that sort of thing—at least not at this point. So play with your cards close to the vest for a while. There will be plenty of time later to describe the amazing adventure you've had moving from tongue-tied wallflower to seasoned public speaker.

It's best to start this phase of talking to real people slowly, just as you did with your isolated practice in the shower. For example, you might start with your own family at the dinner table. Look through the newspaper or a recent magazine and find a story that is full of human-interest details and doesn't try to be funny, preachy, or persuasive. The account should be inherently interesting or unusual because of its content, not because it depends heavily on clever storytelling techniques, such as the use of dialect or a tricky finish. A good example might be a feature story about a high school kid who became a top softball pitcher in spite of the fact that he was born without hands. He taught himself to "throw" the ball from a balanced position on top of his right foot. As you're relating the incident, by the way, don't stand up—just sit there informally as you always do in normal dinner-table conversation.

The subject you choose should have enough length in the telling—perhaps a couple of minutes—so that there is an opening, a middle, and a strong finish. And your telling of the story should be continuous until its completion. As you summarize the incident, you may well find all eyes locked on you in rapt attention. You'll begin at that moment, and perhaps for the first time in your life, to know what it's like to be a speaker holding the interest of an audience. Try this technique for a few weeks.

Next, you should try to vary your "secret speaking" projects by choosing more difficult topics and then moving outside your family to try out your budding talents on friends and acquaintances you don't know quite as well. Before you get together with these outsiders, though, you may want to spend some extra time planning what you want to talk about. One approach might be to look over some recent magazine article or newspaper you've read and pick out one news story with an interesting sequence of events and one editorial or "opinion piece." Study them more closely than you normally do and then, on a separate piece of paper, jot down what you consider to be the three or four most important points or facts in each article. Finally, note your *opinion* of the event or editoral viewpoint you've read about.

Under no circumstances should you omit this last opinion-forming stage in your preparation! It's absolutely essential that an effective speaker have a definite position—a clear-cut set of convictions on the subject he's talking about. If you don't believe in what you're saying, you can't be a truly effective public speaker.

It will also be helpful to go over, *out loud*, the points and brief opinions you've written down for both the news story and the editorial. Then practice your "secret speeches" a second and third time out loud, just to be sure you can express yourself fairly smoothly. At this stage keep your talking short—only two or three minutes for your

17

description of each article. With the news article you'll be getting some practice telling some kind of brief story—perhaps how hostages were kidnapped overseas, or how the President made a fool of himself on a political trip. With the editorial, you're more likely to be summarizing a line of argument about some pressing social or political issue.

When you've finished your third dry run for each article, you're ready to get together with your friend. But remember: You're still not at the stage where you want to play the role of a fullblown public speaker. So sit down at the table with him, act natural, and talk about whatever you normally talk about for a few minutes. Then try your news story on him.

You might ask, "Say, did you read about that hostage situation in Brazil?"

If he says yes, don't let that stop you—the chances are he hasn't studied the article as closely as you did. Launch right into your brief one- to two-minute description of the event and tell him what you thought of it. Then give him time to respond and let the conversation drift in the direction that interests the two of you most. Then, at the next lull, bring up the subject treated by the editorial and go through your description and analysis of the article.

Do you see what you're doing? You're giving yourself valuable experience in stringing together several coherent sentences and then capping them off with an opinion or conclusion. In effect, you're delivering mini-speeches without facing the threat of standing up before an audience. I'd suggest that you try at least a half dozen of these "secret speeches" before you go on to the next step in developing your own personal public speaking style. And keep on making them, even after you've started giving actual speeches before groups! You can use as much practice as you can get in presenting your thoughts orally to others. And the added attraction to this "secret speech" approach with friends is that you're sure to become a much more adept or interesting conversationalist with family and friends if you prepare a little for what you want to say.

The next stage in your secret speaking, which will draw you one step closer to making a real talk, is to try standing up when you speak to your family or friends. Don't be theatrical or inappropriate about it. Pick a time when it's natural for you to be on your feet, such as when you're standing around with other people at a party or when the time seems right to stand up and stretch after you've been sitting a while. You might even get up and propose a toast on the subject you've selected to talk about.

Above all, don't be impatient with remaining in any of these secret speaking stages for a period of time. These are plateaus in your learning curve, and you should be satisfied to stay right where you are for a few weeks or even months until you get over the self-consciousness of speaking for several straight minutes, both in a seat and on your feet. Try telling the same stories several times to different "at home" kinds of audiences so that you can develop a "feel" for where the emphasis should go at different points in your narration.

Also, although reading the reactions of your audience is an advanced subject that will be discussed much later in this book, I think it's appropriate to alert you right here to the existence of the feeling that an experienced speaker can get from his audience. Any group of listeners is like a single person in many ways. They will exhibit the same attitudes of unease, boredom, and even hostility that an individual does. Part of this reaction can be sensed almost psychically by the speaker, and part becomes evident by loss of eye contact, coughing, shuffling of feet, whispering, and sudden exits by different people.

The time to start learning to "take the temperature" of your listeners is right there in your own private audience of friends and family. Get into the habit of watching them critically while you're talking, to see if and where they show signs of inattention. Their eyes may start glazing over when you go into technical details that are boring, too lengthy, or irrelevant. Or maybe you've reached the climax of your story too early: The curtain has, in effect, gone down, but you're still onstage! Or your entire story may be ill-chosen to begin with and doesn't merit their attention.

Every audience, large or small, tells the speaker how he's doing. You don't have to wait for some "Nielsen report" to come to you from a computer when you're a public speaker. Imagine you're a handball player when you're standing in front of a group. Every idea you throw out and every comment you make is a ball you've hit toward the audience, who represent the front wall of the court. If the ball doesn't come back to you—if there's no bounce of expectancy or approval from your listeners—you'll know you've flubbed it.

Even the beginning speaker, and perhaps I should say *especially* the beginning speaker, should be alerted to watch for every sign of interest and every flagging of attention. Then, as you become better at reading your audience, get used to changing, shortening, or punching-up your basic story material on the spot to regain their attention.

The final preparatory step you should take before you confront a real audience is to get a tape recorder and, in private, record one of the "secret speech" presentations you plan to give to one of your friends. I've saved this step until last because most people get so discouraged at the sound of their own voice that they just give up any thought of becoming a competent speaker. You may discover to your horror that you have a nasal twang or an abrasive, high-pitched edge to your voice. Or you may hear yourself saying "you know" or "uhhh" every other breath. Don't despair! Almost everybody has a few speaking flaws. We all tend to get sloppy in casual conversation, and that sloppiness spills over into our more formal, public presentations. But if you've heard yourself on the recorder, be thankful you have had the chance to discover privately any annoying speech characteristics. If you listen to yourself in a variety of situations—such as rehearsing a "secret speech" or engaging another person in an actual conversation—the impact of hearing yourself on tape will be much more useful than any number of corrections by another individual. When you hear your own voice, it hits you! But keep in mind that *you can change*! You can alter your oral delivery just as you can build muscles by doing certain forms of exercise.

But to build your "speech muscles" more effectively, it's necessary to move beyond your secret speeches and try a few talks before a real audience. I've found the best, least threatening way to put the public into your public speaking is, first, to try some informal speaking games in the warmth of your own family circle.

CHAPTER THREE

🪆 🪆 🪆

The Forensic Family

T he time is fast approaching for you to "come out of the closet" as a speaker. Up to this point, you've practiced some public speaking techniques either by using your imagination in an isolated location, such as a shower or an actual closet, or you've talked in the presence of friends and family members without informing them about what you're up to.

But as your spouse, children, parents, or siblings see you speaking more freely and relating interesting accounts about news events, it's likely that somebody will finally ask, "How come you're telling us all these stories? You never did this before!"

When the question comes, be forthright and candid. Confess that you're practicing on them because you're studying a book on public speaking, and they're part of the first step in the learning process. Even if they don't bring up the subject, you should eventually tell them what you're doing and then immediately suggest that they join you in some speaking games that can be a lot of fun for gatherings of a family or close friends.

Now, I'm aware that even in the closest circle of friends or family members, the fright of communicating in even the simplest way can strangle all creative juices—especially if you present the activity as a "performance" or "public speaking" venture. You've probably attended a family party where everyone was having a good time playing, laughing, and kidding, and then somebody pulled out a movie camera and announced, "Okay, everybody, just keep on doing what you're doing! I'm going to take some candid pictures of the family."

This declaration will automatically deprive every single person in the room of the ability to act naturally. Everybody freezes for a moment and then the most unnatural, phony acting begins to take place. Normal emotions become forced, laughter becomes shrill, and physical movements get jerky. And this is happening in your *own* living room, where only your own family is involved!

The way to avoid this sort of strained atmosphere is to present your public speaking practice as a parlor game, like Scrabble or Monopoly. And be sure you don't even mention the phrase "public speaking," or you're likely to get few volunteers. Remember that public speaking is the chief fear, not only for you, but probably for everybody else among your family and friends. Here are four speaking games I've found to be a lot of fun—and also very helpful in developing speaking skills.

The Crazy Storyteller.

I was introduced to this exercise in a public speaking course in high school, and I've since used it in my own family many times. Here's how it works. You sit down for a few minutes and come up with some outlandish topics for stories, such as "Mermaids I Have Dated" or "Why Coconuts Have Hair." Then have everybody gather around in a circle. Throw out one of these topics to each person in turn and ask him to make up a story about it. None of the topics should be disclosed in advance so that everybody has to speak entirely off-the-cuff, without any prior preparation.

At first, there are likely to be a few long pauses or blank looks, but soon most people will get into the swing of things, and the resulting crazy stories will be truly hilarious. For example, I was hit with the "Why Coconuts Have Hair" topic in that high school class, and here was my response:

"Originally, as everyone knows, coconuts did not have hair. They grew much as they do now, but without any hairy overlay. In those days, the climate of the world was quite warm and pleasant, but then the Ice Age moved across the world and drastically lowered the temperatures so that animals and vegetation had to adapt or perish. Many kinds of tropical fruit they had in those days are gone now because of the severe cold, but we still have coconuts because they grew hair. They lasted through the cold winters and icy weather quite well, and when the glaciers finally left, the coconuts liked their hair so much that they decided to keep it—even though they didn't need it anymore. So that's why coconuts now have hair!"

This story is complete fiction, of course, but a game like this gives you practice in telling a short story as fluently as possible and thinking fast on your feet to get from one part of the story to the next. Each person might come up with a different procedure in making up a story like this, but my own method is to decide immediately what conclusion I want to reach. For the coconut story, hair suggested warmth to me, and that gave me a theme around which to organize my talk. When you follow this method, at least you know where you're going to end up, and the more often you tell stories like this, the more smoothly you're able to fill in the middle part of the story.

There don't need to be any winners or losers in this sort of game, but you might want to hand out some favors or trinkets if you're using the game at a real party. For example, you might have one prize for the funniest story, one for the most plausible, one for the most inspiring, one for the most persuasive, and so on. I used to employ exercises like this one during the warm-up on "People Are Funny," before we went on the air. The audience would really begin to get excited as different people tried their hands at storytelling, and we often screened our contestants according to who could do the best job of talking off-the-cuff on topics like these.

Continue the Story.

Our own kids had a great deal of fun with this game when they were younger, and the experience they got in thinking fast helped them become much more articulate in later life. In this game, I would throw out a topic like "My Day on the Amazon River" and then start to tell a story:

"Thirty-five years ago, I was thrown out of a canoe into a river filled with piranha. I started swimming as fast as I could toward some falls that were just ahead of me—because I knew piranha hate falls. Then I went over the falls and found I was safe from the piranha—but I was hurtling down an eighty-foot drop toward some jagged rocks."

Then I might look over at my son, Jack, and say, "You continue the story!" It would be up to him to come up with a solution to the dangerous rocks and then carry the story on to another difficult problem where another family member would pick it up.

This sort of game also gives you the speech-making skills of becoming articulate, thinking quickly on your feet, and developing your imagination without casting the whole experience in terms of making a formal speech. There's a play attitude that predominates, and the threatening prospect of having someone say, "Okay, stand up and make a speech," has been bypassed.

The Interview Game.

My business was interviewing kids when I was doing radio and television programs a number of years ago, and I used to practice by interviewing my own kids. The practice sessions became so enjoyable that they became an end in themselves and a really fun way for the entire family to pass an evening together.

This game starts out like the others. You come up with several provocative topics, such as, "You're a big game hunter who has just returned with the biggest elephant tusks in history." Then you announce a topic, point to one of your family members, and start asking questions. Set a time limit on the interview, such as three minutes, and cram as much conversation as you can into the allotted period. Here's the way the interrogation might go:

"When did you first see the big fella?"

"What were you armed with?"

"How many shots did it take to bring him down?"

"How did you know he was dead?"

"Did he chase you through the jungle?"

"How do you go about skinning an elephant?"

"How do you get the tusks off?"

"How much did they weigh?"

"How much will you get for them?"

"What are they going to be used for?"

The idea is to keep pouring the questions on, one after the other with as little hesitation between each as possible. Obviously, there is almost as much pressure on the interviewer as on the person being interviewed. Each must think quickly, and different speaking skills can be developed, depending on which side a person takes. The one asking the questions has to avoid redundancies and concentrate on coming up with interesting, succinct, hard-hitting questions. The person on the other side has to do most of the talking and must learn to deliver a coherent, persuasive explanation in response to his interrogator.

Here is another topic that might elicit funny responses in this game: "You have just been arrested for doing ninety miles an hour going the wrong way down the sidewalk on a one-way street." The questions might go like this:

"Why were you driving that fast?"

"How did you get on the sidewalk of the one-way street?"

"Did you hurt anybody?"

"How did you happen to have beer on your breath?"

Another subject that has resulted in gales of laughter at a number of family gatherings is, "You're a salesman going from door to door, your questioner is the lady of the house, and you're trying to sell her a live cow." Some sample questions:

"What do I want a cow for?"

"How big is the cow?"

"How much milk does it give?"

"Can you give me some lessons on how to milk a cow?"

"How does the milk get into the cow?"

The variations on topics like these are limitless, and the main fun is often just in listening to people work their way through the question-and-answer sessions. I generally prefer to have the adults in the family take the role of questioner and the kids step into the shoes of interviewee because the one answering the questions usually has to do most of the talking. I think the more practice children get at this, the more articulate they'll become in later life. Too many parents diminish their kids' speaking capacities right from the beginning by failing to give them opportunities to speak informally on different subjects. Or parents may unintentionally frighten their children by asking them to make a kind of formal speech in front of guests, rather than by sneaking up on speech making in the guise of a game.

I've seen so many children blossom with a great sense of humor as they come up with an imaginative explanation for the "invention of bloomers" or "how the President of the U.S. can get rid of taxes." But too often they're embarrassed or even scared by a parent who demands, "You haven't said much, Johnny. Don't be so tongue-tied! Why don't you tell us what you did at school today?" Then a silence settles as everybody waits for Johnny to perform; and more often than not, he freezes or refuses to speak on command about a topic he's not particularly interested in or prepared to talk about. A few such experiences like this, and Johnny, and every other normal child, begins to respond negatively to all public speaking situations. He's well on his way to becoming deathly afraid of talking before any group on any topic.

The Sixty-Second Speech.

This game is one that can be fun for any age group and can also fine-tune your sense of how long it takes you to tell certain kinds of stories or make a series of points before a group. The main idea is to assign a person at the back of the room to hold a watch with a second hand and keep track of how long different people in the group talk. Each talker should try to time his conversation so that he stops as close to the sixty-second mark as he can. You can assign crazy topics for this game just as you did with the other exercises, or you can just let the person make up a story as he goes along. Also, it's often fun to arrange the sixty-second test in the form of an interview, with a leader asking the questions and the person who is supposed to be stopping the clock doing the answering.

I can remember a situation involving one woman I tried this on during a radio program a number of years ago. The exercise was set up in the form of a game, and I told her, "You tell me when you think a minute is up, and if you're within five seconds either way, you'll get a mink coat." It seemed like a rather simple task to her, as I began to ask her questions like "Where did you meet your husband?" and "Where would you like to take a trip if you could go anywhere in the world?" She got so absorbed in our conversation that she completely lost track of time. I finally had to remind her after two or three minutes had gone by that we were in the middle of a contest, and she replied, "Oh my goodness, I got so interested in what you were saying, I forgot all about the time!"

When a person is talking by himself, without being asked any questions, though, the opposite usually occurs. He thinks a minute is up when only about twenty to twenty-five seconds have passed. In other words, when you're straining to think of something to say, time goes by a lot slower than you think it does. It takes a considerable amount of practice and speaking experience to estimate fairly accurately how long you've talked. But, after a while, you'll find you can come pretty close in this sixty-second game. I've worked on radio and TV and before audiences so many years that I have a kind of clock in my head now. I've found I can come within two to three seconds most times.

These are just a few of the games you and your family and friends might want to try to improve your speaking skills. As I've mentioned, you can award prizes for "winners" if you like, or you can just stage these games for the fun of the personal interaction, without any winners or losers. Personally, I think it's much less threatening for inexperienced speakers if you avoid prizes, at least at first. When everybody gets comfortable with the various games, you might make a few of the exercises more competitive by giving token awards.

After you've spent some time getting used to expressing yourself orally with these exercises and games, you'll probably start getting more curious about what it would be like to deliver a real speech. Even the briefest thought of giving a more formal talk will cause many of you to begin to tremble. Your stomach will feel like it's moving up into your mouth, and your hands will get clammy and shaky. But don't start running in the opposite direction! Some of the best speakers experience these feelings of nervous distress—even after they've given hundreds of talks before groups of all sizes. You can learn to control your nervousness—I'll go into that subject in more detail a little later. The important thing to keep in mind is that, through your various "secret speeches" and other exercises, you're much better prepared now than you were a few weeks ago to give a formal talk. So let's plunge right into the nuts and bolts of how to organize and deliver a basic public speech.

PART II

❦ ❦ ❦

How to Organize and Deliver a Basic Public Speech

CHAPTER FOUR

☘ ☘ ☘

The Basic Ingredients

Most people give mediocre speeches for two reasons:

1. They don't spend enough time *organizing* their research
2. They fail to *simplify* the information they're trying to communicate.

You'll notice I didn't say people give bad speeches because of a lack of research. Some certainly do fall short for this reason, but most of the time, if you're scared of standing up in front of a group, you're going to go overboard in gathering material. In other words, the basic facts you need to give a good speech are at your fingertips. You just don't know how to take the most fundamental step in preparation—fitting all the facts and figures together into an interesting package. That's the main problem I want to address in this chapter.

There are six key ingredients that have to go into an effective public speech. Leave any one of them out, and you're likely to end up with the same sort of bland mess you'd get in the kitchen if you forgot to put the apples in apple pie. The first three of these elements deal with researching your speech, and the second three relate to organizing it.

Ingredient 1:
Boil your subject down to one short sentence.

Every good speech has a crystal-clear theme, one that can be stated easily in a phrase or short sentence. For example, you might decide you're going to talk about "The Five Common Houseplants That Are Most Dangerous to Children" or "How the Immoral Habits of the Royal Family Caused the Decline of the British Empire" or "How Jogging in Jerusalem Made the Holy Land Come Alive for Me."

In other words, you should have a concrete enough idea of the basic theme of your speech that you can respond clearly and confidently if someone asks, "What's your topic today?" Vague statements of your theme often reflect fuzzy thinking or a failure to hone in on the exact points you want to make. Beware if you have to fish around to describe your topic or if you find yourself giving an abstract, vague response like "I'm speaking about interesting buildings in America." If you can't get any more specific than that, you're probably well on your way to delivering one big yawn of a talk.

One of the best ways I've found for being sure I've got a definite theme nailed down is to grill my personal contact in the group I'm speaking to. I might ask, "What exactly would you like me to talk about?" Or, "I can discuss X, Y, and Z pretty thoroughly—do those topics interest you?" If the representative of the organization has trouble getting specific, I might ask a series of questions about the kind of audience he expects to attend, their occupational and avocational interests, what other speakers have talked about, which speeches seemed to interest listeners most, and what specific activities the organization engages in besides just listening to me speak.

Spending some time finding out this information is one of the most important kinds of research you can do for a speech. And the more you know about what the audience expects of you, the more definite and interesting a theme you'll be able to come up with.

Ingredient 2:
Build a firm but fascinating foundation of facts and figures.

I'm not suggesting that you have to spend several weeks digging up enough information to write a doctoral dissertation! Just spend enough time, maybe less than an hour, gathering a sufficient factual and statistical under- pinning to enable you to speak with some authority on your subject. But the crux of your talk, when you're just starting out as a public speaker, should be based primarily on your own personal experience and knowledge of your subject. I don't think a beginning public speaker should *ever* talk about something that mainly comes out of the public library. Whatever research you do should only *back up* your own highly personal understanding of your topic.

One of the best and quickest ways to get this sort of "back-up" information is to check the periodical index in your local library for relevant articles in reputable newspapers and magazines. Well-documented publications like the *New York Times*, *Washington Post*, *Los Angeles Times*, *Wall Street Journal*, *Fortune*, and *Psychology Today* will suit your purposes just fine. If you can get your figures from original sources like the Bureau of Labor Statistics, publications by research organizations like the Gallup or Harris polls, or in-depth treatments in books, so much the better. But again, don't put all your energy into digging up a set of comprehensive but obscure facts that may bog you down and divert your attention from the other essential ingredients of speech preparation.

It's also important as you're gathering these hard, cold facts and figures to realize that you have to "warm them up" somehow. You might try using words instead of numbers if you're dealing with percentages (e.g., "one out of five" instead of "twenty percent"), and the more frequently you can inject a personal note into a statistic, the more likely you'll be to keep your audience listening closely to you.

George Gallup, Jr., the president of the Gallup Poll, uses a veritable avalanche of statistics in most of his talks. Yet he's in constant demand as a speaker, in part because he knows how to marshal his facts in a way that is highly personal and relevant to his audience. He gave one talk on "Religion in the 1980s" to an audience of several hundred at the Park Avenue United Methodist Church in Manhattan, and he reeled off one set of percentages after another: "Ninety-four percent of Americans believe in God," "more than eight of every ten people believe in the divinity of Christ," and so on. Yet he kept his audience sufficiently on the edge of their seats so that one listener was heard to remark afterward, "I could have listened to him for another half hour!"

His secret? He varied his presentation of his survey findings and also concentrated on making them personal. Instead of constantly using the word "percent," he frequently said, "one out of three people" or "one American in five." And each time he stated a numerical fact, he related it to the interests of his audience: "A big failing in our churches is that they are not providing concrete ways for your people to express their social concern and their need to help others"—this remark being made in a church that had just presented the first performance of a junior choir. Or, "The main-line denominations are losing members, and two of the main ways they might reverse this trend are to emphasize Bible study and focus on a deeper understanding of Jesus Christ." Appropriately, the people to whom he was speaking were members of a "main-line" denomination, the United Methodist, and the tendency of many of Gallup's listeners was to *personalize* his words and try to decide, "Does what he's saying apply to me? If so, what can I do about it?"

But as important as facts and figures are, you can't sustain an audience's interest with them alone. It takes the third ingredient, several fascinating illustrations and stories, to round out your research for an effective speech.

Ingredient 3:
Find some fascinating yarns to spin.

Good illustrative stories are the cement that can help you pull together a really successful speech. In fact, I think a good rule of thumb is that the more stories you tell in a speech, the better—and I'm not talking about humorous stories. The best way to make a hard-hitting point in a talk is to use a short anecdote to illustrate what you're trying to communicate.

Generally speaking, I'd recommend that amateur speakers stick to short stories. Get to the point as quickly as possible and then move on to the next phase of your speech. The average story should probably take about a minute and a half to tell, and should almost always run at least a minute. Anything shorter usually wouldn't qualify as a full-fledged anecdote. You have to allow yourself enough time to set the stage, relate the narrative of your story, then wrap everything up in a concluding statement so that your listeners understand exactly how your anecdote fits into the main theme of your speech.

Just as a good story has a minimum time limit, it also shouldn't run on too long, especially if you're giving a relatively short speech of fifteen or twenty minutes. The longer your story runs, the better it has to be, so it's best to protect yourself and have an improved chance of keeping your audience's attention with something short. I'd recommend that you limit all your illustrative anecdotes to no more than two minutes in a fifteen-minute speech, and I'd have one story ready to illustrate each major point in your speech. In other words, if you have five major points in your fifteen-minute speech, you should tell five stories, each between one and two minutes.

For example, if you're giving a speech about the

importance of excellence and quality in daily work, one of your points might be the idea that "excellence will always win out, even against difficult odds." To illustrate this point, you could use a story like this:

"A number of years ago, there was a very timid man who had a problem with stuttering and was petrified by the idea of going out and meeting the public. But he had a creative mind and possessed certain technical skills. He saw that the different kinds of brushes that were being sold in the stores were of what he considered to be inferior quality. So he started spending all his extra time inventing a better brush, and finally he succeeded.

"But now he faced a problem. He had a superior product, but he had few prospects of *selling* his product because he was not a good communicator. Still, he didn't let his inadequacies hold him back. He started knocking on the doors of strangers, but rather than trying to persuade householders to buy his products by verbal means, he let the brushes speak for themselves. He spent more time sweeping floors, scrubbing glassware, and scratching backs with back brushes than he did talking.

"And the brushes sold themselves. This shy inventor, whose name was Alfred Fuller, proved beyond doubt that 'excellence will win out' as his superior products paved the way for the great Fuller Brush success story."

By my calculations, this story takes a little less than a minute to relate—though your pace of delivery may be somewhat faster or slower than my own. I should offer one word of caution here, though. The above story is written out completely, but I don't think it's a good practice for you to read from a script when you're speaking to a group. An outline or notes of some sort are preferable so that you can effect a more natural delivery, but we'll get into this subject in more detail later. For our present purposes, I just wanted to let you see what a typical story might look like if it were written out verbatim.

The important thing to remember here is that a story will be more memorable for your listeners than a series of abstract points because we human beings are all natural storytellers and story listeners. It's much easier to remember a point if it's connected to a yarn about a little girl who ran away from her mother than it is to remember the five steps necessary to sell a widget if none of those five points are related to some sort of anecdote.

So if you expect to do an increasing amount of public speaking, start looking for interesting stories in newspapers, magazines, and other written sources. Clip them out and keep them on file under appropriate headings, and you'll find your speech preparation time will be cut at least in half.

These three elements in putting together a basic speech are related to research—to gathering the facts you'll try to communicate to your audience. The next three ingredients may be even more important, though, because they will be decisive in determining how well you organize those facts for the greatest impact on your listeners.

Ingredient 4:
Get off to a fast start.

The way you start a speech can determine how well you deliver it and what kind of ultimate impression you make on your audience. So I think it's generally smart to devote as much time to preparing your opening remarks as to any other part of your speech. You should know your opening lines absolutely cold, and you should go over and over them to get just the right pace and inflection. And above all, keep your opening simple! I'm often reminded of a situation I faced daily in interviewing children on my radio and television programs. I'd get a little girl or boy up on the stage, with cameras and lights distracting the child, several hundred unfamiliar people rustling in the studio audience, the unseen presence of an invisible coast-to-coast television audience, and microphones moving about. Under those circumstances, I'd know it would be quite easy for any kid to lose his sense of composure and freeze up if we didn't get started on the right foot. So the first thing I'd do would be to get him to say something that was very safe and simple, just to get the words coming. And the simplest thing anybody can do is to tell who he is.

So I'd usually begin by asking, "What's your name?"

The answer would always come rather easily: "I'm Johnny Smith." And that was the trickle of verbal water that would prime the pump.

Then I'd go on to something else almost as simple: "What's your daddy do?" And the conversation would start to flow.

The same principles apply to you, as a beginning or inexperienced speaker. Don't try to bowl your audience over with a joke or a tricky story with a surprise ending! If you fall into this trap, you're almost certain to spend the rest of your talk trying to extricate yourself. Speak simply and straightforwardly from the outset, and you'll find the words will start coming and your audience will warm up much more quickly.

Another important principle to keep in mind when preparing your introduction is that it's essential to establish a point of identity with your audience right at the beginning. A good talk is like a play with a prologue. And a good speech always has the same theme in the prologue: You should mention something about yourself that will enable your listeners to think, "He's one of us!"

For example, you might say, "I feel very much at home tonight with this Kiwanis Club because in my home town, if you needed to have anything done, you always asked the Kiwanis Club to help. Ever since I can remember they were there planting trees, getting children on the milk fund, and supporting other worthwhile projects. So I'm especially happy to be able to share this evening with you. . . ."

With this sort of approach, you've complimented your audience and identified your own values and interests with theirs. Sometimes, it's also possible to combine your first remarks about the subject of your speech with your words of personal identification. But don't worry too much if you can't mesh the two together all the time. Some topics and audiences are easy to put together this way, and some aren't.

But if you've limited your prologue to words of identification that help you relate to your audience, the next thing you have to do is to get into your subject. I'd strongly advise you to do this with some dramatic, arresting statement that does a strong, simple job of presenting the basic theme you formulated in Ingredient 1. If you can grab their attention right at the outset, they'll probably stay with you until you close. If you have a weak or vague opening, though, you'll find yourself trying to keep your head above water until you sit down.

Here are a few suggestions about how you might formulate an opening:

- "Many of you here may not know that as you sit in this hotel right now, with the kind of gas connections that the local plumbers' union is using, we could all be blown sky-high any moment!" (This could be the end of your talk if you have a skittish audience!)

- "I'm happy to be here at the PTA meeting because I've had three children, and I know the trials and tribulations the average parent sitting out there has. And what I'm here to talk to you about is one of the biggest problems we parents face—vandalism. Vandalism by your kids and their friends takes two dollars out of your pocket every week because that's the amount of additional taxes that are levied across the county for repairing the schools that have been damaged and replacing those that are burned down each year." (You can see that this opening combines both the prologue of audience identification and a dramatic introduction of your subject matter.)
- "Enjoy your clothes, cars, and home appliances while you can because in a few years they're going to be exorbitantly expensive . . . if they exist at all! The synthetic materials and fuels that go into so many of our ordinary goods are becoming more and more scarce because those synthetics and fuels come from petroleum, and petroleum will become virtually unavailable to ordinary Americans in the next decade." (This opening illustrates one of the key ways to get an audience's attention: by raising an issue that affects their pocketbooks.)

In newspaper parlance, this opening for a story is called a "lead," and many publications pride themselves on coming up with such colorful leads that they can hold most readers throughout an entire article. Your goal as a speaker should be similar to those newspaper writers, as you sit down to dream up a good opening. Put yourself in the audience and imagine what would make you sit up and take notice if a speaker were speaking on your topic. Usually, if you focus on some sort of "pocketbook" issue—a point that directly affects their personal finances, safety, or emotional well-being—you'll be off on the right foot at the start.

Ingredient 5:
Search for a well-shaped body.

The second part of a speech, which comprises the main part of what you have to say, is often referred to as the "body." And just like a physical body, the body of a speech isn't likely to inspire much interest if it's in "bad shape"—that is, if it's poorly organized.

First of all, when you're organizing the body of your talk, always keep yout time limit—and the limited attention span of your audience—in mind. In some cases you may not have much choice about how long you speak. The group that wants to hear from you may say, "Make it a half hour," or, "We've set aside forty-five minutes to hear your views on such-and-such a subject."

More often, you'll be given some leeway: "Oh, take the time you need, but our speakers generally run anywhere from a half hour to forty-five minutes." If you're given a broad range of time in which to speak, it's important to remember that your audience has a limited attention span. We live our lives in twenty- to thirty-minute segments, in part because that's the time it takes to sit through a typical situation comedy on television, plus the usual number of commercials. So I'd say that if you have a choice, it's safest to keep your remarks to twenty or thirty minutes if you

46

want the best chance of keeping the interest of the largest number of your listeners.

When you speak up to forty or forty-five minutes, you've got to have some very good material. To talk for a full hour, you have to be a very good speaker, in addition to having good material. And to hold your audience for an hour and a half—about the length of many feature motion pictures these days—you really have to be a stem-winder!

After you've settled on the length of your speech, the next step in organizing the body is to isolate three to five clear main points you want to make and then categorize all your illustrations and facts and figures under those points. The stories and facts should be chosen carefully so that they further or strengthen the argument you're trying to make. If you throw in irrelevant stories or figures, your audience will immediately pick up this flaw and decide, "This guy is disorganized!"

Also, each of your main points should be related back *explicitly* to your main theme. You may think that it's obvious that certain stories make a certain point and relate back clearly to your main speech topic and that therefore it's not necessary for you to belabor the obvious. Don't fall into this trap! Some mediocre speeches could be transformed into good or even superior talks if the speaker would just insert a few phrases and sentences as verbal signposts or markers to direct the thinking of his listeners back to the main thread. *Remember:* You're much more familiar with your subject matter than your audience is, so don't assume they know even half as much as you do.

As an illustration of this concept of relating stories and facts back to your main theme, imagine you're a dentist giving a talk to a group of lay people about "The Dentist as

Amateur Psychologist." You give an interesting opening and then make a couple of points about experiences you've had helping adults train their minds to eliminate feelings of pain. But then you launch out on this story:

"Kids in the dentist chair are really a problem. I can show you a finger that was almost bitten off when I was feeling for a loose tooth. This one kid was sitting in the chair, and I couldn't get him to open his mouth, no matter how much I coaxed him. As he was sitting there with teeth clenched, I looked up on my wall and saw three certificates proclaiming me to be an expert in various phases of dentistry, but nowhere, in all my years of education, had I been taught how to get a child to open his mouth. But then I hit upon a scheme. . . ."

And you proceed to tell how you got the child to open his mouth, and also how he bit you.

If you stop there, you may have succeeded in telling a fairly interesting story, but you will have failed to tie your story back solidly into your main theme. In other words, it's important to end the anecdote with something like ". . . and that's how I learned to be a child psychologist." It may seem obvious to you that the audience will make the leap from your story to inferring that the story illustrates your progress in becoming an amateur psychologist, which is your basic topic. But to your listeners, it may not be obvious at all. They're processing a great deal of unfamiliar information while you're speaking, and you have to make it as easy and clear for them as possible.

So always remember to organize rigorously, clarify every concept you're communicating, and tie in each of your points with your main theme. If you follow these principles, you'll succeed in fashioning a well-shaped body for your speech.

Ingredient 6:
Know when and how to stop.

One of the surest ways to spoil a good speech is to trail off for five to ten minutes after you should have wrapped the whole thing up and sat down. Limit your concluding remarks to a minute or two at most, and then end it! If you keep on going, savoring the great job you've done, your audience will quickly tire and you'll be enmeshed in an anticlimax that will leave them with a bad taste in their mouths. One common pattern for ending a speech is to summarize each of your main points briefly, indicate some future prospects for the subject you've spoken on, recite a brief poem or quotation that sums up your feelings on the topic—and then give them a smile and a wave and walk away!

If these six ingredients are present in your speech, you'll have the basic framework you need to capture and hold the interest of almost any audience you meet. But there are many little tricks and flourishes that any inexperienced speaker can quickly master to put a near-professional veneer on his presentation. The first of these I'd like to introduce you to is the most tantalizing, and also the most difficult—how to tell a joke to an audience.

CHAPTER FIVE

The Non-Joke-Teller's Guide to Telling Jokes

The best advice I can give you as you're trying to launch yourself as a successful public speaker is this: Don't tell jokes!

This may seem strange advice, coming from a person who loves a good laugh and who believes wholeheartedly in a positive-thinking approach to life. But I know how easy it is for an amateur to get into serious trouble with bad jokes on a speaker's platform. Joke-telling is the riskiest, least understood, and highest paid of the performing arts because jokes require timing, inflection, authority, and native skill that most people don't possess.

But if you're like most people, I haven't discouraged

you yet. You still want to learn how to tell a joke. So rather than allow you to bungle your way through a series of bad jokes and ruin perfectly good speeches you may have prepared, I'm going to share with you some inside tips I've picked up over the years, both in performing and speaking myself and in watching other good joke-tellers in action. I've arranged these tips into what might be called "the nine key guidelines for getting a laugh," and here they are.

1. Choose your jokes to suit your personality.

Your personality generally suits you for telling only certain jokes effectively. In fact, even top professional comics are extremely choosy in incorporating certain kinds of jokes into their routines and discarding others.

I've seen Bob Hope take twenty-two pages of jokes from eight top humor writers and with a pen he'll read down the list, check one, jump past three, and check another. Out of the entire group of jokes, he might pick about one-third for possible use and then reject the others, even though some people might think all of them were hilarious.

I asked Bob about his selection procedure, and he said, "There's nothing wrong with this joke," pointing to one that he decided not to use. "But I just don't visualize myself doing it. That isn't the kind of routine I can 'lay on' or 'hit' as well as some of the others."

In other words, even though all the jokes handed to him might be funny, he knows which *he* can sell, and that's a very subjective thing. Each person's personality and background suit him to tell certain jokes effectively and put him at a disadvantage with others. You have to learn by trial and error which kinds of humor you can put over and which you should stay away from.

I used to argue with my own radio and TV writers about this subject because some would begin to feel personally insulted when I'd fail to use some of their material. I'd say, "Fellows, I'm not arguing with you about how good or bad that joke is. I'm just saying I don't like it for myself, and if I don't like it as a performer, I'm not going to do it well." When you're in front of an audience, you need confidence more than anything else—you need to know you can do the best job possible of delivering funny stories. If you don't have that confidence, you're not going to be very funny.

As you pick your own jokes, you might also keep in mind this distinction: It's been said that there are two kinds of people who can get a laugh: (1) people who say funny things; and (2) people who "say things funny."

I'm more inclined to say funny things, and I think most people, including those of you who are reading this book, are potentially in this category. But some people have such a natural clowning instinct that it really doesn't much matter whether the stories they tell are inherently funny. They can get a laugh just in the way they relate an anecdote. Ed Wynn, for example, could tell a mediocre joke and turn it into something hilarious, and Jonathan Winters, with his imitations and funny noises, can provoke belly laughs from material that wouldn't even cause a smile if someone else were saying it.

But perhaps the best person I've come across in "telling things funny" is Danny Thomas. He can take a long story or joke and in the manner of telling it, he can build it into a hilarious listening experience. His most famous story is the "jack" story, which goes something like this: It seems this fellow has a flat tire on a deserted road and finds he doesn't have a jack. But he sees a light down the road and starts walking toward it. As he's trudging along, he begins to think all these negative thoughts: "It's just my luck that when I get there, the man in that house will be asleep . . . and he won't be at all happy about being waked up . . . and it will start to rain and I'll get drenched as I'm standing outside talking to him . . . and then the guy will get mad at me . . . and in the end, he'll decide he doesn't want to give me a jack. . . ."

Finally, when the motorist rings the doorbell, the homeowner barely has time to stick his head out the window before the driver yells angrily, "You can take your jack and stick it!" But the punch line is only the frosting on the cake. By the time Danny gets the man to the house (which may take him fifteen minutes), the audience is practically rolling on the floor because of the funny way he's built the story to a climax.

Danny Thomas is a master of telling stories funny, but I would advise you to stay away from this or any other difficult style of joke-telling unless you find you have a special knack for keeping people laughing. But if you discover you can do certain kinds of jokes well because you naturally have a funny way of doing a dialect or gesturing or otherwise clowning around, by all means select your jokes with these native abilities in mind.

2. Take out an "insurance policy" on your jokes.

Because you're rather inexperienced telling jokes in front of anyone, much less an audience of strangers, it's important to get some "insurance," something to fall back on in case your attempt at humor doesn't go over very well.

There are two types of joke insurance that I frequently use, even though I've spent a lifetime fine-tuning my own joke-telling skills. The first type might be called "famous authority insurance" because it involves attributing your joke to some well-known comic or humorist. You might say, "This reminds me of a story Will Rogers used to tell. . . ." Or your authority might be Bob Hope or Rodney Dangerfield or anybody else you like. Then, after putting responsibility for the joke on this other individual's shoulders, go ahead and tell it. Your audience will feel receptive to a "big name" joke. Then, too, if you don't get a laugh, you'll at least *share* the blame with the famous comic. After all, the joke came from him, not you; so if it's no good, it's his fault, not yours!

The second kind of joke insurance might be called the "meaningful point" type. The idea here is to tell the funny story or joke *not* just to get a laugh but also to make a point that furthers the main argument of your speech. For example, if you're talking about how pessimistic you are about the direction of world events, you might say, "The world situation is so bad I can't decide whether to watch the early news on TV and be unable to eat, or the late news and be unable to sleep!" Now, you might get a few titters or even a laugh from this one-liner, depending on the audience you're speaking to, but even if you get blank stares, you've at least made the point that you're not happy about what's happening in the world. In other words, you've insured yourself against falling flat on your face. You may stumble a little, but you won't go down completely.

You're in a much safer position using this joke insurance in your talks than comics like Bob Hope and

Johnny Carson are; they *have* to be funny. Nobody expects you to keep everybody rolling in the aisles, and if you can come up with a few mildly amusing remarks or stories, most of your listeners will probably be pleasantly surprised. The main idea is never to try to hit a "home run" with your jokes, such as by trying to tell an obvious joke, with no subsidiary serious point, at the very beginning of your speech. You should also avoid leading off with a statement like, "I heard this really hilarious joke I want to share with you. . . ." Once you've committed yourself like that, you have no choice but to hit them right in their funny bone; and if you miss, you've not only failed to hit that home run but you've struck out. So limit your objectives in joke-telling, at least at the beginning. To carry the baseball analogy all the way through, be satisfied with a "walk" or a "single" rather than a "home run." If you can just get on base with your audience, and move them gradually toward the major objectives you're trying to accomplish in your talk, you'll be more likely to come up with a winning game as a beginning speaker.

3. If you must make up a joke, make fun of yourself.

Writing jokes is a highly specialized art that requires years of experience to perfect, so don't assume you can sit down and make up your own jokes. You may come up with a genuinely funny idea, but unless you know how to pace the telling of the story, weed out all extraneous verbiage, and otherwise polish it to a professional tone, you're not going to be able to get the humor across.

The best sources for funny material that amateurs can

use in talks are magazines with good joke sections like the *Reader's Digest* or books with huge collections of funny stories, many of which you can find in your local library or in a good bookstore.

But sometimes you may come across an amusing incident that actually occurred and has never been committed to paper, and it's possible that you just might get a laugh out of it if you can hit upon the right approach of relating it to an audience. One ironclad rule I'd suggest you follow if you must make up your own joke is that you tell the joke on yourself. People are always more willing to laugh at something stupid the speaker himself did than they are at things he says that ridicule or poke fun at others.

For example, if you've been asked to speak about how to set up a health insurance program in a corporation because you're supposed to be something of an expert on this subject, you might start out with a semi-apologetic kind of personal joke: "I'm not sure I'm the best one to talk to you about this topic because the other day I couldn't even find my own Blue Cross card, which I'd left in a wallet, which was on the seat of a car, which got towed away to the police station . . . after I'd backed up over my mother-in-law!" Using an accumulated buildup of disasters that may have happened to you like this can often get the audience laughing with you.

One variation on this personal-joke approach, which is somewhat more dangerous for the beginning speaker but which I've used successfully on a number of occasions, is to say during the first part of your speech: "To begin my talk tonight, I suppose I should tell you a funny thing that happened to me on the way to this dinner because every time I go to a dinner like this the speaker always says, 'The funniest thing happened to me on the way to this dinner.' But you know, ladies and gentlemen, I have been going to events like this for twenty years, and *nothing* funny has *ever* happened to me on the way to a dinner . . . until tonight."

I say this approach is dangerous for a couple of reasons. In the first place, the joke is positioned toward the first part of your speech, and as we've already seen, a joke that fails early in your talk can put you at a decided disadvantage. Also, you're telling the audience you think what you're about to say is funny, and that can be very dangerous if you tell a bad joke.

At the same time, this technique has several possible "insurance policies" that can be attached to it. First, you're personalizing the joke, and people are always more likely to laugh at something silly you did rather than at something that happened to somebody else. Also, you can get a laugh just out of that introduction if you pace it properly. For instance, I would probably stress the phrase "twenty years" by raising the tone of my voice slightly and then use a slight pause, as indicated by the ellipsis points, just between "dinner" and "until." The phrase "until tonight" is a surprise the audience won't be expecting, and as we'll see in Guideline 4, surprise is a key element in every good joke. So if you can pace this introduction to your joke properly, you'll start out with some sort of a laugh, and there won't be so much pressure to get a big laugh on the joke itself.

Finally, I would strongly suggest that you attach still another insurance policy to the main joke about what happened to you on the way to the dinner. Probably the strongest insurance would be to tell an anecdote that makes a meaningful point, and perhaps even signal to the audience that the main reason you're telling the anecdote is that you want to make a certain point. In other words, you might say, "Actually, what happened to me is more instructive to illustrate something important I want to tell you tonight, rather than being particularly funny." Then, if you get a laugh with the anecdote, you're in a stronger position than ever because you will have told *two* funny things and provided an important illustration for your listeners on top of that.

But let me emphasize one more thing about this issue of telling jokes on yourself rather than on others. If you tell a good story on somebody that no one in the audience knows, you may well get a good laugh and leave the audience with good feelings toward you. But if you make fun of somebody they *do* know, such as one of the those listening to you, you're sure to get in hot water—even if you get a laugh.

I'm reminded of a young man I know who started doing some serious speaking while he was still in high school. He managed to give one speech that, almost by accident, provoked gales of laughter from the entire student body. His subject was a summer he had spent with a family in Europe, and he quite seriously began to describe the differences in customs between that family and his own—such as the fact that his European hosts took baths only once every couple of weeks and, as far as he knew, they never changed the sheets on his bed in the eight weeks that he stayed with them. To his surprise, the audience thought the description was hilarious, and by the time he had finished he had firmly established his reputation as a campus humorist.

Unfortunately, this fellow didn't understand exactly *why* he had been so funny, and he made the mistake of thinking he could get a good laugh no matter what he said in front of a group. One of his teachers reinforced this misconception by saying, "You know, you're really a funny speaker. How would you like to give a light, humorous talk at a dinner we're having for some former students when they return for a reunion in a couple of weeks?"

The would-be humorist accepted and was quite confident he could make as big a hit with this second group as he had with the first. He knew that many of those attending the reunion were students at a local military college and they had been required to shave their heads after they enrolled, so he made up a couple of jokes—or what he thought were jokes—about the many bald heads in the audience: "The spotlight is bouncing off so many polished skinheads out there, I can't read my notes!" Well, not only did he alienate the military students, who were rather defensive about their hairdos, but he also succeeded in annoying some of the older members of the audience, who were losing their hair because of advancing age.

The mistake this young man made is that he made fun of the wrong people; even if he had managed to get a few laughs, many of his listeners would have left with a sour taste in their mouths. As a matter of fact, this student's problem was rather similar to a problem I faced when I was much younger. Many people are afraid of standing up to talk before a group, but that was never my main concern. I always loved to clown around and ham it up in front of an audience. And the larger the audience was, the better I liked it.

The big flaw in my early public speaking style was that I was by nature a smart aleck. I found it quite easy to get a quick laugh by making fun of other people, and I didn't hesitate to use this ability whenever I got the chance, whether it was in a public assembly of the school, a debate, or a classroom discussion. I can still remember one debate before a rather large audience in which I spent a lot of time concentrating on the personal characteristics of my opponent rather than on the issues. I said, "How can you believe anything from a guy who would wear a pair of pants like my opponent apparently exhumed from the attic?" Or, "I suppose my opponent may be making a good argument, but with his grasp of the English language, he couldn't sell a fire extinguisher to Joan of Arc!"

As a kid, I got some laughs by hitting out with a verbal bludgeon, instead of using a rapier, until a couple of my teachers criticized me for my insensitivity. One, a junior high principal named John Aseltine, said, "Art, you want people to like you, don't you? Well, people who are bleeding from your sarcastic blows aren't going to like you. You have a God-given oral ability, and it isn't fair to get up and hurt people who don't have it. They can't always defend themselves, and you're becoming a bully with words."

I realized that even though I might be able to get a cheap laugh by calling somebody a "needle nose" in public, I was really hurting myself in the long run. The laughs I was getting were sometimes more nervous titters than anything else because my listeners were just expressing some relief that they had been spared for the moment from my sharp tongue. It was at this point of realizing I was doing myself more harm than good with my verbal cruelty that I began to learn more about more constructive humor.

4. Every good joke springs a surprise.

Almost all effective jokes have an element of surprise, a verbal banana peel that flips your listeners over in an unexpected direction just as it appears you've been leading them in another.

A good illustration of this principle is a story a seven-year-old boy told me on one of my shows—without even realizing he was making a classic joke. I asked him, "Were you born here in California?"

"No," he replied. "We moved here from Kansas City four months ago."

"Why did you move to Los Angeles?"

"My daddy wanted to see if he liked it."

"How *do* you like it?"

"We're moving back next week!"

The little boy's last line is the surprise element, an unexpected way of saying, "We don't like California." When you're choosing your jokes, always look for the surprise twist, and be sure you feel it's distinctive and funny. If you're not particularly inspired or caught off guard by the final punch line, the chances are your audience won't be either.

Another strength of this little boy's joke is the fact that it's short and to the point—and that's the next key guideline for joke-telling I want to discuss with you.

5. Short jokes strengthen your speech.

The converse of this principle is that long jokes may destroy your speech. The longer your "funny" story runs on, the stronger finish you have to make. If you take a minute or more to tell a joke, you're asking your listeners to invest a great deal of time, and the more time a person invests, the more he expects to get back at the end.

I like to think in terms of a five-point scale in evaluating jokes according to their length. One point should be assigned to every ten seconds it takes you to tell your joke so that a twenty-second joke is a "two-pointer," a thirty-second one is a "three-pointer," and so on. There are many good jokes you can tell in fifteen to twenty seconds, but when you move past a half minute, you'd better start hearing some warning signals in your head. A three-point, or thirty-second joke, may be relatively safe, but anything longer than that should be truly a superior side-splitter. And if you find yourself going on for as much as fifty seconds (a five-point joke), you'd better be sure you're a super storyteller and also have some interesting, funny little angles as you're progressing toward your ultimate punch line. In fact, you should probably be able to "tell a story funny," the way we saw Danny Thomas do it in the first guideline, before you venture past the one- or two-minute limit.

It's important to distinguish, by the way, between *joke*-telling—which should usually be kept shorter than thirty seconds for the beginner—and *story*telling to illustrate a major point in your speech. As we've already seen in a previous chapter, a serious, inspirational, or instructive anecdote should always be at least a minute long and should probably average about a minute and a half. But that's because the main thing you're trying to do with your anecdotes is paint illustrative pictures to explain your concepts to your audience; your primary purpose is not to get people to laugh.

6. Learn all you can about laughter.

Many people can't tell a good joke because they don't handle the punch line adeptly. They may rush through it too quickly or otherwise play it down because they lack the confidence that they can really get a laugh. That's a sure route to failure. If you're going to tell a joke, you have to go for the laugh aggressively, or it's best not to try to tell jokes at all. In other words, move smoothly up to the funny surprise in your story and then with a pause or wide-open eyes or a big grin—or whatever other emphasis seems appropriate—deliver your punch line strongly, then give your audience a moment to laugh.

If they don't laugh—and you have to be prepared for that sort of dead reaction because it happens even to the most experienced joke-tellers—then pick up your speech line quickly and go on to your next point. Although you have to use a strong finish if you hope to get a laugh, it's not necessary to anticipate a *big* laugh. If you tell your joke and then stand back for too long waiting for a ripple of guffaws, and nothing happens, you may get disconcerted and completely lose track of where you are in your speech.

In a normal speaking situation this sort of loss of composure won't happen to me because I've experienced most problems with joke-telling. Also, I know how to "save" a funny routine when one of my stories doesn't go over as I had hoped. But there's one unusual type of audience I've always had trouble telling jokes to, and that's one composed of people of different nationalities who are listening to me over translation headphones. The last time I confronted this difficulty was at the United Nations when George Bush arranged for me to talk about drug abuse to various international delegations. I was introduced by Secretary General U Thant and decided to illustrate one of my points with a funny story. But I hadn't taken into account the fact that there were several dozen different languages into which my talk was being translated, and each of those translations was occurring at a different place and therefore had a different length. So I told the joke, delivered the punch line strongly, and then stood back and waited for the laugh I was sure was going to come. There was silence: a terrible moment of silence. Then gales of laughter started coming from the various delegations one by one—first the Norwegians, then the French, then the Germans . . . and finally the English.

As a speaker, one piece of inside information about laughter you should know is that only about one out of every three people actually laughs out loud at a joke. So even though your story may not result in audible howls and chuckles, that doesn't mean you weren't funny. It may just be that you're speaking to a relatively small group with not enough "laughers" present to express their amusement out loud. I recall going to an occasional dinner at the Hillcrest Country Club in Los Angeles where top comics like Milton Berle, George Burns, George Jessel, and Henny Youngman sometimes sit around a table and try out their new material on one another. You may have eight of these people sitting around listening to jokes, and they rarely laugh out loud. They just beat the table or the air with outstretched hand if somebody tells a good joke.

7. Steer clear of dangerous jokes.

I've already warned you about not trying to tell jokes that make fun of other real people, especially those personally known to people in your audience. But there are other dangerous waters you should avoid.

It's best to avoid jokes about politics, religion, or ethnic minorities—unless you're a member of the group you're making fun of. I tell a great many religious stories, but I always introduce the joke by reminding the audience that I'm a preacher's kid and a Baptist. I can even tell jokes about Methodists, provided I do it as a Baptist in a good-natured tone. For example, "I can't understand why the Methodists always wonder about how so many Baptists get into heaven. After all, the guy guarding the gate, St. Peter, was a Baptist, wasn't he?"

But the only way I can comfortably tell a Jewish joke is to be sure that the Jewish person comes out ahead. If I tried to tell any other kind of Jewish story, I would be flirting with disaster because I wouldn't be poking fun at my own tradition but at someone else's. Jewish comedians, on the other hand, can tell almost any Jewish joke they like because they're laughing at themselves.

Also, I never tell a dirty joke or even a slightly off-color one. If there is any doubt in my mind, I discard the joke completely because I don't see any point in irritating even one person in a crowd that may number in the thousands. There are plenty of clean jokes. Why take a chance?

But even this clear-cut policy of mine doesn't always keep me out of hot water. A letter recently came across my desk from a man who wrote, "I brought my young son to hear you at a positive-thinking rally a couple of weeks ago, and I was absolutely astounded to hear you use the word 'damn.' I have always told my son never to use that word, and here you were, the hero of the entire event, saying 'damn.' "

I had said "damn" not offhandedly but to make a point in a story I told, and if I hadn't used it, the anecdote would have been much weaker. Yet I believe it's best to avoid even as mild a word as "damn" rather than take a chance on alienating anybody. Telling dirty jokes and using profanity can be a seductive thing because a certain segment of many

66

audiences will always howl at off-color jokes. I know several comedians who have fallen into this trap, but they eventually find that even though they are getting cheap laughs, they are hurting their reputations with the larger family crowd. They begin speaking to increasingly narrow audiences. Also, as often as not, people will join the crowd and laugh at your dirty jokes and then, on their way home, they'll criticize you for telling them. So stay away from this sort of humor. Stick to clean jokes and you'll find you're a much more popular speaker.

8. Take advantage of ad-libs.

One of the funniest and safest ways to make a joke is to pick up on something unexpected or even disruptive that happens as you get up to speak or while you are speaking. For example, if you're asked to say a few words at the birthday party of your ninety-year-old grandmother as they're lighting the candles, you might quip, "I'm glad you're not one hundred today, Granny, or we might have to call the fire department to get a permit for the extra candles on that cake!"

If this remark were obviously a prepared joke, it might not be particularly funny. But in the context of the festivities, it could get some big laughs.

Any halfway decent pleasantry, if it's clearly off-the-cuff, always has a much better chance of amusing an audience than a prepared story. I often look for chances to make spur-of-the-moment comments as I get up to speak—such as those times when the person introducing me stumbles over my name. My remarks don't have to be strong at all to absolutely kill them because everyone knows I'm ad-libbing and they automatically give me credit for that.

9. Practice, practice, practice!

Good prepared jokes are constructed like a small, tightly built brick house. If you get one brick—one word or pause or inflection—out of place, the whole thing will be crooked. So as you're preparing jokes for a speech, go over them several times to cut out excess verbiage or alter phrases you can't deliver naturally. And try out your jokes on at least three people to see how they react. If you don't get any laughs during these dry runs, drop the jokes and look for some others. Finally, be sure you have the punch line memorized down pat and that you've worked out the best way of delivering it. If you aren't on top of this final, key part of the joke and you stumble over the words—or worst of all, you forget them—you'll bore rather than amuse your listeners.

I can't guarantee that if you follow all these guidelines, you'll always get a belly laugh. But I do believe you'll score with jokes more than you strike out. As I said at the beginning of this section, it's probably best to avoid telling jokes altogether because attempts at humor always involve greater risks than delivering a straight, serious speech. But a good joke or two can liven up any talk, so if you're inclined to take a stab at some light, funny remarks, don't let me discourage you. You may have the next Johnny Carson hiding behind that sober exterior of yours!

CHAPTER SIX

⚓ ⚓ ⚓

Nerves of Steel

S ome nervous tension is absolutely essential to a good speech. If you feel nothing unusual inside when you stand up before an audience, you're probably on the verge of delivering one of the world's all-time terrible talks.

The best kind of nervousness is a heightened sense of your powers—perhaps something akin to the anticipation an Olympic athlete feels as he gets ready to run a big race. I look forward to that kind of edginess because I know it signals the possibility of a highly effective address. But sometimes your fear of facing an audience can begin to get the better of you and either adversely affect your presentation or at least take all the personal joy out of it for you.

Don't despair if you get the shakes at the mere thought of getting up before a group. As far as I can tell, every great speaker has gotten nervous at some point, and many top talkers *always* experience something close to an anxiety attack.

To illustrate just how bad a case of nerves even top performers can get, let me tell you a story about Harry Einstein, one of the very best old-time comics. He performed under the stage name "Parkya Karcass" and was known as "Parky" to his show business friends. I had been asked to serve as toastmaster at a banquet honoring Lucille Ball and Desi Arnaz. It was one of Hollywood's most prestigious affairs, and everybody who was anybody was there. There were eighteen top stars on the dais. Parky originally had been a furniture salesman in New England and got a reputation for telling funny stories so hilariously at his business meetings that he finally got an offer to go into show business and became a star of the Eddie Cantor show. He was giving a particularly funny talk that night, and as he spoke, Lucy—that consummate star of stars— leaned over to me and said, "Art, I'd give anything to be able to be as calm as he is, giving a speech like that."

I was a little surprised because Lucy is so great in situation comedies, but I also knew many of our great performing artists are frightened to death of public speaking. And I also knew something she didn't know about Parky.

"Lucy," I replied, "I happen to know Parky has not eaten lunch or dinner, and his stomach has been churning for the last four hours. Under that calm facade, he's dying!"

"I can't believe it!" she said, shaking her head.

Parky soon finished his routine and sat down to wild applause. I walked back to the microphone and said,

"Parky, you were never better. You should have your own prime-time hour on one of the three networks."

He looked up at me, smiled, put his head on Milton Berle's shoulder, and died on the spot. The tension he constantly lived under had finally taken its ultimate toll. We carried him backstage and quickly brought the tragic evening to a close.

I tell this story, not to frighten you away from becoming a public speaker, but rather to suggest that no matter how nervous you feel, you can still give a good speech if you learn how to control that nervousness and channel it. Or as I've said in another context, it's okay to have the butterflies in your stomach if you can get them to fly in formation.

One fine speaker who has learned to make his butterflies fly in formation is Charlton Heston. He has conquered the world as Moses and in other majestic movie roles, but he doesn't rely just on ordinary preparation and his naturally imposing public presence to get him through a speech. He always excuses himself about twenty minutes before he is scheduled to face an audience and retires to a private room where he meditates and communes with himself until someone comes to tell him it's time for him to go on.

The lesson for you to learn from Heston's technique is that if you find you get confused and rattled when you have to move directly from your seat to the lectern without any opportunity to collect your thoughts, then ask your hosts to set a room or alcove aside for you so that you can do some last-minute preparation before you speak. The need to take a few final minutes to get calm and organized is nothing to be ashamed of. If Charlton Heston can do it, so can you!

Another way to achieve this last-minute control over your nerves is an approach used by Dr. Norman Vincent

Peale. Despite his broad experience and great reputation as an inspiring speaker, he still gets what he calls "the same old fluttery feeling" he had when he was petrified of public speaking as a boy. But, like Charlton Heston, he too has found a way to make his butterflies fly in formation.

"What I do is I say, 'Come on, Norman, get with it!' " he explained. "I say, 'Get with it, forget yourself! You are not important. Love those people out there and believe that the Lord will help you. Now get out there and start talking!' I really give myself a working over as I'm sitting on the platform or as I'm waiting in the wings. The wings are the most frightening place because you're back there by yourself, just before you've got to step out before this big crowd. I follow this approach even for my Sunday sermon in church. I say, 'God help me to get out there and do it!' I give myself a swift mental kick."

Dr. Peale isn't the only major religious figure ever to get a case of the nerves in his public speaking. The Old Testament tells us that having received a divine command to appear before the Egyptians, Moses himself argued with God, "O Lord, I have never been eloquent, neither in the past nor since you have spoken to your servant. I am slow of speech and tongue."

God replied: "Who gave man his mouth? Who makes him deaf or dumb? Who gives him sight or makes him blind? Is it not I, the Lord? Now go; I will help you speak and will teach you what to say" (Exodus 4:10–12, New International Version).

Moses still had cold feet and tried to beg off this assignment, so God told him He would arrange for Moses' brother, Aaron, to do the talking. Moses, in other words, let his nerves get the better of him; but there's no reason for you to do the same. There are inner resources and practical procedures you can employ to harness your shaky feelings,

72

and I want to go into more detail with you about those techniques now.

It's been years since I felt at all jittery about standing up to speak to any sort of audience, but there once was a time when I had more trouble with my stomach butterflies. In fact, I used to tell a joke about my nervousness that went like this:

I'd say, "I enjoy being here and I may look calm and collected—but I must confess that I was washing my hands at a sink backstage a few minutes ago, and a lady walked up to me and asked, 'Are you Art Linkletter?' I said 'Yes,' and she said, 'Are you nervous?' I said, 'No, what makes you think I'm nervous?' and she said, 'Then what are you doing in the ladies' room?' "

But jittery nerves have never been a major problem for me because I've always loved to speak. The main feeling I get now is one of exhilaration, or great anticipation so that I can hardly wait to get out there. If the fellow introducing me is drawing out his remarks, I start pacing and muttering, "Hurry up and get it over with! Get me on!"

In fact, I'm so calm that at a banquet appearance, I'll continue to eat right up to the second that the person introducing me says, "Art Linkletter." Then I'll put my fork down, swallow my last bite of cherry pie, and say "Good evening" without so much as a gulp. But I don't expect you to be so casual about the speech-making process. After all, I've had decades of experience doing this sort of thing, and I make my living now as a professional speaker. You're not a professional, and you don't want to be one. You just want some "first-aid" principles that will get you over that occasional talk and the accompanying nervousness. So let me share with you a few personal principles that I believe have reduced my own tendency to be jittery and, more important, are applicable to your situation.

⚹ Do your homework.

If you know you're on top of your subject, you're much more likely to feel comfortable standing up before a group than if you've thrown some things together at the last minute. You don't even have to present your materials in a highly polished way to do an adequate job. Certainly, if you hope to do an above-average job, you should follow the basic ingredients of a speech, including good organization, that we discussed in Chapter Four. But if you've at least got the facts, even if your presentation isn't that skilled, the chances are your audience will respond well. And if you know they are likely to respond well, there's that much less reason for you to feel nervous.

⚹ Practice your entire speech several times.

Many amateur speakers I know think they can outline a speech on paper and then stand up before a crowd to deliver it without going over it out loud beforehand. That's a serious misconception of what public speaking is all about. There's a basic difference between *writing* and *speaking*, and it's important for you always to keep that distinction in mind. I've been asked on several occasions if certain speeches I've given could be printed in different magazines, but I find when I look over the transcript of what I've said, the manuscript is often unpublishable. The speech itself may have been excellent, but when written out as I spoke it, it doesn't make a suitable article.

So you're likely to find that the notes or outlines you make of your speech have to be altered and fine-tuned before the speech is ready for an oral delivery, and the only way to be sure your talk will go smoothly is to go over it several times out loud. I've recommended using a tape recorder to work out some of your basic speaking defects and to get used to the sound of your own voice. But a recorder can also be a big asset as you practice your speech. As you listen to your own voice on tape, you can tell more easily how smooth your transitions are from one part of your speech to the next, how effectively you're using the tone and volume of your voice, and how clearly you're communicating the important points.

Don't become a perfectionist in your speech making.

One of the greatest sources of frustration—and nervousness—in public speaking is to start believing you have to do a perfect job every time you stand up before a group. I always try to do *my best under the circumstances*, but I don't allow myself to worry about matters that go beyond my capabilities or control. This attitude gives me a greater sense of perspective on each talk I give and allows me to relax, shrug, and in effect say to myself, "That's the way it goes" if anything goes wrong.

And things frequently *do* go wrong—in my public appearances as well as in the experience of every other professional speaker. I can remember one incident that might have reduced an amateur to a quivering bundle of nerves but which I was able to take in stride because of my refusal to fall prey to the pressures of perfectionism. I had been invited to speak at the United Way drive in Detroit, and the major assembly, a picnic meal, had been scheduled at a Ford plant there. As I was sitting next to Henry Ford and Mrs. Ford on the platform, with about five thousand people finishing up their dinners before us, I noticed some of the maintenance staff and other officials scurrying around on the stage.

"There seems to be some problem," I commented.

"It's the public address system—it's not working!" somebody exclaimed.

I went back to my food and continued to chat with Mrs. Ford on some other topic until she interrupted me: "You don't seem to be at all worried about the public address system!"

"No," I replied. "I'm concerned, but not worried."

"But what will you do?"

"I'll go home."

"You'll go home?" she said, alarm now creeping into her voice.

"There's nothing else for me to do," I explained. "First of all, I can't fix the system because I know nothing about the mechanics of it. Second, I can't speak without it before such a huge crowd. It's kind of like sitting in an airport, and if the pilot announces, 'The engine just fell off the airplane,' there's nothing you can do. You just don't go."

"That certainly is a calm attitude," she said.

"What else can I do?" I asked. "I'm sure your husband will speak to the people in charge, and everything that can be done will be done—including the invention of a new public address system."

And it was. Swarms of men came into the place, and I don't know what they did, but a few minutes later the public address system was working fine.

Because of their greater experience, professional speakers may be more likely to assume this sort of attitude than those who are less experienced, but there's really no reason why you, as an amateur, can't also get a sense of perspective this way. Just prepare as well as you can, and if things out of your control start going wrong, tell yourself to take on an attitude of detachment and relax. It's obvious that you can't do better than your best, and if you allow an unhealthy perfectionism to start distorting the realities of speaking situations you face, you'll never learn to make those nervous butterflies in your stomach fly in formation!

Some of these personal insights about overcoming nervousness that I've acquired through practical speaking experience have been confirmed, with a few new twists, in formal psychological research. Dr. Bradley Bucher, associate professor of psychology at the University of Western Ontario in Canada, has conducted extensive experiments in behavior-changing techniques, and he suggests the following procedure to reduce your tendency to be anxious when speaking before a group.

Dr. Bucher says there are three basic sources of anxiety related to public speaking: (1) the physical basis for anxiety in your inner muscles; (2) your inner perception, or "feelings" about your nervousness; and (3) your lack of speaking skills. He says that the first two sources of speaking anxiety can be overcome by a psychological process known as "desensitization," and the third can be attacked through a systematic training program to increase your basic speaking abilities. Let's examine each of his recommended programs in turn to see how they fit into our understanding of effective public speaking for private (and nervous) people.

Desensitization involves, first, either imagining or doing certain relatively easy things associated with your anxiety about speaking, then progressively trying harder activities. The main idea is that as you progress from easy to harder tasks in the public speaking "hierarchy" of skills, the more you tend to reduce the anxiety you feel with the harder tasks. In other words, you become "desensitized" or get less sensitive to the nervousness you ordinarily associate with tougher speaking assignments. For example, right now you may get almost apoplectic at the idea of speaking before a group of one hundred strangers. But if you start off with ten strangers, then try twenty, and *gradually* move up to one hundred, you'll find yourself becoming "desensitized' to the anxiety you used to associate with the bigger group.

This program is basically the same as the one I suggested earlier when I advised you to start off by yourself in a shower, then move to a mirror, and so on. But Dr. Bucher puts the procedure in to a more detailed series of steps that I think may be helpful for you to incorporate if you're having a particularly bad problem with nervousness.

Step 1:
Try some relaxing exercises before each speech.

For example, you might try the simple procedure of tightening up each of the large muscle groups in your body and then consciously relaxing each group. This routine isn't going to eliminate your anxiety, but it serves as a helpful "warm-up" to your effort to overcome your nervousness.

Step 2:
Set up a hierarchy of public speaking challenges.

On a scale of one to a hundred, list every speaking experience you think you might conceivably encounter.

Number one would be the easiest, such as delivering a "secret speech" to your family. On the other hand, delivering an address to a thousand of your business colleagues might get close to a one hundred rating. One way to set up such a hierarchy is to spend an hour or so imagining different speaking situations and evaluating how much anxiety you experience just in the imagining process.

Step 3:
Move slowly up the hierarchy.

Start at the bottom of the public speaking "hierarchy" you've created and begin working your way up.

"You might spend a few days asking strange clerks in stores for directions—if that experience is one of the things that gives you anxiety," Dr. Bucher explains. "Then after you can do this without much discomfort, go on to the next step up the ladder. If you find you don't carry off one of the assignments very well, you may have taken too large a step. So back up and try something less difficult. The important thing is to go through the process slowly and gradually. If you decide too soon that 'a speech at London's Hyde Park or the Boston Common is the befitting challenge for me!' you may get so discouraged you won't want to continue with your public speaking at all."

This three-step desensitization procedure will help you reduce the emotional and physical roots of your nervousness. But speaking anxiety can also result from your awareness that you're simply not a very skilled speaker. Perhaps you have nervous twitches or other physical problems, or maybe you're just not preparing your speeches well enough because the anxiety you feel is hurting your concentration. To remedy these practical deficiencies, Dr. Bucher recommends a three-pronged training program:

Find a good public speaking model.

This model, he says, can be an individual who is a more experienced speaker than you are, a good public speaking course, or an instructive book (hopefully, like this one).

Practice well in advance what you learn from the model.

I've been trying to hammer this point into your brain throughout this book. Practice is a key element in your overall preparation of a speech. But Dr. Bucher has also found that preparing and organizing your speech *well in advance* of the scheduled time for the talk can go a long way toward reducing your nervousness.

"Many people get so worried about public speaking that they can't calm themselves down enough to do adequate research and organization," he explains. "One of the reasons for this is that a person may wait until the last minute to try to organize his thoughts, but we've found the closer you get to an anxiety-producing event, the greater and more debilitating your anxiety becomes."

In other words, if you wait until a day or so before your speech to pull your thoughts together, you may find you're so shaky inside you can't concentrate. The obvious solution to the problem, Dr. Bucher says, is to start your preparation

80

and practice far in advance, when your anxiety level is much lower.

Get some feedback.

Feedback about how you're doing as a speaker is "very important," Dr. Bucher says. But unfortunately, most people don't actively look for criticism of their presentations.

"Take lecturers in college," the psychologist says. "It's not surprising that styles of lecturers don't change from year to year because they don't hear when they're doing well and when they're not. In many schools, it's considered ill-mannered for students to give their professors direct feedback, and the only way they have to signal their displeasure may be just to fall asleep or read a newspaper in class. But I think feedback is really the critical element in improving your public speaking."

To get some feedback for your own public speaking and thereby reduce your nervousness by increasing your skills, go to the family member or friend you consider the most objective. Tell him to let you know first what you've done right and then what you've done wrong. And emphasize: "It's absolutely essential that you really be honest in telling me about my faults—otherwise I won't develop as a speaker!"

So no matter how jittery you feel now—how hopelessly nervous you may get before a talk—you *can* master that anxiety and deliver a good speech. I don't care whose method you choose—mine, Charlton Heston's, Dr. Norman Vincent Peale's, or Dr. Bradley Bucher's. The point is that you can find a solution that fits your peculiar variety of nervousness if you just keep experimenting. Don't give up until those butterflies inside your stomach are flying in perfect formation!

⚓ ⚓ ⚓

CHAPTER SEVEN

Making Friends
with
Your Audience

One of the main reasons you feel afraid when you step up to speak before a group is that you are assuming, down deep, that those people out there are your *enemies*. You believe they're sitting there thinking, "What can this jerk tell me that I don't already know?" Or, "This guy certainly *looks* like the biggest bore of all time—now just let him prove otherwise!"

In other words, you probably begin all your speeches by automatically throwing up a barrier between yourself and your audience—a barrier that is *completely unnecessary*. You see, the large majority of those people sitting out there have come to hear you because they *want* to hear you.

Perhaps it's *not* you but your topic that they want to know more about. Or they are inherently favorably disposed toward what you have to say because you've been endorsed by the group that's sponsoring your talk—and they believe wholeheartedly in what that group stands for.

The point I'm making is that you're already ahead of the game before you ever open your mouth. The audience is waiting expectantly to hear you. You're *not* behind any forensic eight ball, even though you may think you are.

One way to impress on your mind the fact that your audience is predisposed for you, rather than against you, is to imagine that they're reaching out to you, or giving you a V-for-victory sign, or smiling benevolently at you (even if you don't actually see a smile on any face). And remember: You're not fooling yourself with this kind of fantasy. Those people in front of you really are looking forward to what you have to say, and almost anything you tell them, no matter how ineptly, will give them some degree of satisfaction.

Your audience genuinely wants to get to know you and become your friend, in part because you're a relatively important person. After all, you're the only one among them that day who is distinguished enough to have been asked to speak. The trick for you is to learn to build on that friendship, to solidify it during your talk to the point where you've strengthened what you've said through the force of your amiable personality.

As an aid in relating more effectively to my listeners, I've come up with a checklist of basic principles for establishing a firm friendship with an audience. I go over these eight points consciously or subconsciously for every speech I make, and I'd also recommend you look them over as you're preparing your talks.

1. Fit your speaking style to the size of your audience.

A friend of mine was asked to speak to a group of executives that was meeting at a large company's head-quarters in New York. He assumed, without checking, that he would probably be talking to forty or fifty people who would be assembled in front of him in an auditoriumlike room, and he prepared his remarks with these assumptions in mind.

When he arrived at the company to give his talk, he found things were quite different from what he had expected. There were only about ten executives present, and they were seated around a large table in a relatively small conference room. He was offered a seat at the table, and that was the spot from which he was supposed to deliver his talk. He had prepared a twenty-five-minute address, with copious notes, and had expected to have a lectern on which to place them. Instead, he found part of his audience peering over his shoulders, looking at his notes as he spoke from them.

Needless to say, the talk was a disaster. When his listeners saw how many notes he had, they became restless only four or five minutes into his speech and started interrupting him with questions. He couldn't maintain effective personal interaction with such a small group because he had to crane his neck around at those sitting at the far ends of the table—and when he looked around like this, he often lost his place in his notes.

This fellow's experience is a classic case of a person preparing the wrong kind of speech for a small audience. In the first place, the speaker should have ascertained more definitely the number of people he'd be addressing and then adjusted his delivery accordingly. When I'm talking to such a small group, I always plan on sitting down with them so that I can relate more informally to each individual on his level. I might use a few notes, but I'd keep them to a minimum; I'd try to avoid them altogether if possible. Otherwise, you're likely to scare off your listeners or perhaps give them the impression you've prepared the wrong kind of speech for the number present.

I'd probably begin by stressing the informality of the setting: "Rather than make a formal talk to you today, I'd like for us to take advantage of the small size of this group to have some personal interaction on the topic under consideration. First of all, let me take just a few minutes to outline my thoughts on the subject and then we'll have some give-and-take on the points that particularly interest you. . . ."

Then I'd take about five or at the most ten minutes to state my position and throw out a few provocative questions to stimulate a discussion for the rest of my presentation. People in this size group tend to get restless or bored more easily than in a larger group because the small size makes them *expect* to participate. If you don't give them plenty of opportunity to interact with you, they're likely to get frustrated.

I might add, by the way, that a small group like this is one of the most difficult to address because you have to be adept at combining a short, hard-hitting set of preliminary remarks with an informative discussion, which you as the main speaker usually have to lead.

When the size group you're talking to increases to about fifteen or twenty people, you can stand up to give your talk. But unless the number of people exceeds about thirty, I would steer away from the use of a podium or lectern. If you stand behind a lectern, especially if it's made

86

of heavy wood and hides your lower body, you may appear to be too pretentious or stiff before the group.

Now, although I plan to get into this subject in more detail later, let me say a few words at this point about the use of notes in different-size groups. Generally speaking, the smaller the group you're talking to, the more obvious your notes become. In the case of my friend from New York, for example, his use of notes with that small group of ten executives was excruciatingly obvious and distracting. I think the best approach to notes with small and medium-sized groups is just to make no bones about the fact you're using them. You might say, "I'm going to talk about public speaking today, and the first thing I want to tell you about is how to tell jokes." Then you pull out a pad or clipboard with your notes on it and say, "Now let's check off some of the things you should know about jokes." As you make each point, actually make a motion to check off one item.

In a larger group, where you're standing behind a podium, you can hide your notes on the holder provided for them. But when you're sitting around a table in full view of your listeners or standing before a somewhat larger group—but without a lectern—it's impossible to hide any papers or cards you may be using. So be obvious and open about them, and your audience won't be bothered at all by the fact that you're relying on them.

Another important element in your speaking that involves the size of your audience is your gestures. The basic rule to remember is the bigger your audience, the broader your gestures. For example, suppose you're giving a political pep talk to a group of about twenty, and you ask, "Where do you think you'll ever find another man to serve you the way our mayor has?" The appropriate gesture in this situation might be to point an index finger around at your listeners as you make the statement. But if you're speaking to a thousand or more, you might open both your arms out to your sides as you ask, *"Where* do you think . . ." As a general rule, I'd suggest that you broaden your gestures significantly beyond the motions you would use in an intimate conversation when your audience passes the two to three hundred mark.

But regardless of the group's size, the important thing to remember about gestures is to keep them natural. If they become too mechanical as you try to broaden them out with a larger group, you'll lose much more than if you just decide not to gesture at all. Let your arms and hands go loose as you speak and permit them to do what seems most appropriate in view of the point you're trying to make. After you've done some more public speaking, you'll find that certain gestures tend to recur in your talks because you feel comfortable with them. I've noticed that I use a "thoughtful" gesture when I'm trying to convey that attitude to my listeners, a gesture that involves putting my fingers together in front of my body like a church steeple. I might say, "Now let's think about all the ramifications of Proposition 13," and as I'm saying these words, my hands automatically go into the steeple pose to signal to the audience that the time has arrived for some contemplation.

In the previous chapter, it was suggested that you try to get some constructive feedback from a straight-talking spouse or friend. If you have that kind of person observing some of your talks, you might get him to point out distracting gestures you use, such as half-formed, nervous sweeps of your hands or cramming your hands in an unattractive way down into your pockets. I never put my hands in my pockets, by the way, because I think that pose is almost always unflattering to my clothing and my general public image as well.

2. Try to shape the physical setting.

It's not always possible, especially if you're a relatively unknown speaker, to make drastic changes in the physical layout of the place where you're supposed to make your talk. But it pays to make a preliminary visit to the room or auditorium where your speech is scheduled to take place, just to get the feel of the physical setting. The room and your use of it should *encourage* your friendship with your audience, not impair it. You might take a friend along and have him stand at the back of the room while you say a few sentences from the speaker's platform. This way, you'll get some idea about whether you're projecting your voice enough to be heard. Or if there's a microphone, you'll know better how you'll have to modulate your voice to be heard properly.

If there's no lectern in the room when you pay this preliminary visit and you feel you need one for your notes or some other reason, be sure to call up the people who are sponsoring your talk and try to arrange to have one brought to the room on the day you speak. If you can't get them to provide a lectern, at least you'll have some forewarning of the fact that you'll have to speak without one.

Another flaw in the physical setting may be the way your audience is to be seated. If you're scheduled to speak in a huge auditorium and you know it will be only about half full, try to arrange with your hosts to have the audience seated from the front to the back by ushers. When people are allowed to drift in on their own, they invariably find seats from the middle to the rear of the auditorium, and that means you'll have a huge gap of empty seats you have to speak over in order to reach your listeners. This arrangement creates a tremendous problem if you hope to achieve a certain degree of intimacy with the group.

If it's not possible to orchestrate the seating arrangements well in advance, you may have to call the people forward just before you speak—and I wouldn't hesitate to do it. You might say something like this: "I'd like to have you all come down closer to me so I don't have to shout at those back in the last rows. This is a chance for the people in the cheap seats to come down here in the front where it costs more! Come on and try out some of these twelve-dollar seats!" Of course the seats probably all cost the same—or nothing at all—but at least you can make your point in a lighthearted way.

Sometimes there's nothing you can do to alter the seating arrangement, and the best you can do is check the place out and brace yourself for a tough speaking assignment. Perhaps the worst physical setting for a speaker is one that is set up like a ballroom dance floor, where the speaker stands on or near the bandstand with a microphone and there is a huge expanse of space, perhaps seventy feet in each direction, before the tables and people begin. This sort of setup makes it very difficult to establish any meaningful interaction between the speaker and the audience, and it's very easy to lose the attention of your listeners because they're sitting far away from you in conversational groups. Perhaps the best way you can counteract this kind of physical setting is to ask for a microphone with a long cord and then pace back and forth in front of the tables and try to focus intensely on eye-to-eye contact with as many of your listeners as possible. This is a very difficult technique for many inexperienced speakers, though, especially those who feel they have to use notes. So if you feel this approach is a little too advanced for you at this point, grit your teeth and stay back at a stationary position at the bandstand mike.

The next most difficult setting is one in which the audience is spread out in a long thin line, perhaps fourteen rows deep and a hundred yards wide, far out to each side of you. To speak to the entire group, you have to constantly swing your head back and forth, and you can never keep a substantial number of people in your line of vision at any one time. The result may be that no one in the audience feels you're concentrating on him or his group as much as on everyone else; the tendency of many listeners may be to lose interest in what you're saying because they suspect you're not too interested in them. An analogous situation would be if you are talking in a small group of three or four people, but you focus all your attention on only one person. The other two are likely to feel left out and may well drift away to another, more interesting discussion.

The fault with the large, spread-out group is not with you, of course—it's with the way the tables or chairs are arranged. But if you don't take steps to rearrange the setting, you may well be the one who will bear the audience's ire or apathy. So do all you can to get your hosts to set up the room so that your audience will be out in front of you rather than strung out past your peripheral vision to the sides; and try to place them as close to the spot where you'll be speaking as possible.

But the arrangement of the seats isn't the only part of the physical setting you should be concerned about. I also always insist that the places where I speak have a light that shines on my face so that my eyes are illuminated. Otherwise, if my face is dark, the person fifteen rows back probably won't be able to see the expressions on my face adequately. Also, a speaker who drones on in semidarkness has a soporific effect on his listeners and may well find half his audience dozing by the time he gets to his concluding remarks.

One dramatic variation I use with lighting at the huge positive-thinking rallies where I speak isn't necessarily a technique I'd recommend for you since you're not a professional speaker. But I think this approach does highlight how effective proper lighting can be to enhance the impact of the spoken word. First, when I walk onto the stage with fifteen or twenty thousand people waiting to hear me, I am acutely aware that I have to try something a little different to hold their attention. My challenge is that I'm often the final, "anchor leg" speaker who is capping off eight hours of virtuoso performances by several other top professionals.

So I immediately walk right down to the lip of the stage, right into their very laps, where there are no notes, no lecterns, nothing between me and my listeners. The only thing I have to hold on to is a hand microphone. The next thing I do is something that many speakers adamantly avoid doing—I have all the lights in the place turned out except for one heavy "trooper" spotlight that stays trained right on me, hitting me right in the face. I can't see a thing when the blast of light hits me in the eyes. I know there is a sea of thousands of people out there, watching every move and gesture I make, but I have no idea how they're reacting or behaving. For all I know, they could all be filing out of the auditorium while I'm delivering my talk.

I've been asked if I don't go for this theatrical effect because of some macho, "gunslinger" element in my personality that needs to take on the ultimate kind of audience-speaker confrontation. But actually, I feel I *need* to use this approach because the audience has already seen everything there is to see in public speaking performances, and I have to go them one more. They've heard Norman Vincent Peale, Paul Harvey, and a host of other top talkers, and now I've got to give them a little something extra, as a final send-off for the evening. I'm like the final bullfighter who comes out and has to *kneel* as he taunts the bull because everyone else did it standing up.

So I deliver my entire address, from the initial funny lines to the final inspirational thrust—an entire forty-five-minute presentation—with the spotlight glaring down at me and not a hint of how my audience is taking it except for the periodic laughter after a joke and the final ovation.

I'm certainly not suggesting you attempt anything like this—it's taken me years of experience in speaking regularly before large crowds to be able to handle this kind of nerve-racking approach. The point for you to remember is that as you give each of your talks, try to become more sensitive to those factors in the physical setting that help you get your message across, and also those factors that get in your way. It's difficult to make friends with one individual if he can't see you, hear you, or concentrate on you, and the same holds true for your relationships with your audience. So keep an eye out for those physical flaws that annoy or distract your listeners, and do everything you can to eliminate them before you set foot on the speaker's platform.

3. Learn how to use a microphone.

Most inexperienced speakers don't know how to use a mike properly, and if you misuse the mike, you can destroy your entire speech. Because there is a good chance that you'll be using a mike for medium-sized and larger audiences, let me pass on a few tips about how to make an effective speech with a sound system.

First of all, you should at least arrange to say a few words into the microphone before your audience arrives so that you can see just how loud you have to talk to project your voice effectively to every corner of the room. You may also want to experiment with the positioning of the mike if it's the "gooseneck" type or one that can be adjusted up and down according to your height and posture. If the mike is too close, you may get a hissing, spitting sound; if it's too far away, your voice may get lost completely. So try it out until you're satisfied that the equipment has been adjusted to meet your particular physical and voice requirements.

One other big mistake that many amateurs make in using a gooseneck microphone, even after it's been adjusted properly for them, is to forget that when they turn from one side of the audience to the other, they must continue to talk *across* the mike, and not away from it. Here's what I mean: A beginning speaker will say, "Good evening, ladies and gentlemen," and then he'll turn to the left and continue, "There are two main things I want to talk to you about tonight. . . ." But as he turns to the left, he moves only his head so that as he speaks, his mouth is projecting his voice *away* from the mike, rather than into it.

That's the wrong way. The right way to use the mike in this situation would be to rotate the entire upper part of your body slightly to the right as your head rotates slightly to the left. In this way, your mouth and voice will continue to be directed across the mike, rather than away from it. It stands to reason that a stationary microphone won't follow the movement of your head. (The situation is different, of course, if you happen to have a movable mike clipped to the front of your tie or dress.) It's necessary for you to ensure that your head and body move in such a way that you can get the maximum benefit from the mike.

If for some reason you don't have a chance to test the microphone before you start speaking, you might want to say, "Can you hear me all right back there? Just raise your hand if you have any trouble hearing me during this talk." If I've been uncertain about the way my voice is projecting over a mike, I've used this approach myself. It's much better to get some immediate feedback from your audience before your speech rather than learn after you've finished, when it's too late, that a certain segment of your listeners couldn't hear you. Also, showing concern for the audience in this way can help you establish a warmer rapport with them. You're establishing yourself as a concerned person who is solicitous about their welfare, rather than an outsider who is just in a hurry to finish what he has to say and sit down.

But suppose you find people raising their hands after you've made this offer, and you still can't make yourself heard because you've been saddled with a defective microphone?

The problem has confronted me on a number of occasions, and I always place the blame right where it belongs—on the staff that maintains the equipment in the auditorium. This tactic may seem as though I'm pointing the finger too much, but after all, why should I or any other speaker accept responsibility for a situation we didn't create? And with some crowds, you can really catch the brunt of a massive wave of wrath. I've seen people demand their money back, get very angry at the speaker, and totally reject what he has to say just because they couldn't hear.

Once when I was speaking before about eight thousand people, many of whom were grumbling because they couldn't hear me, I said right on the mike, "I'm terribly sorry that many of you can't hear well, but that is the fault of the people who have this auditorium. Please don't blame me. I'm speaking clearly into this microphone, and it's just not working. I would fix it if I could, but I don't have the tools or the expertise to do it."

95

In perhaps the most ludicrous situation I've ever encountered of this sort, I had been asked to fly down to the Bahamas for the opening of a big multimillion-dollar hotel. About a half dozen stars were being paid top dollar to participate in this extravaganza, and they were making us speak and perform over the worst public address system I've ever seen. When I stood up to speak, the first thing I said was, "Isn't it amazing how intelligent, successful builders and architects of hotels can spend $27 million on a gorgeous hotel like this and then put in a public address system that costs $1.74? Asking those of us on this platform to come down and work on this public address system would be like asking Dr. DeBakey to do a heart transplant with a trowel and a pair of pliers!"

Remarks like this may seem a little strong for the audiences you will find you're asked to speak to. Obviously, if you're talking to a low-key, low-budget church group that doesn't have the money to install a sophisticated sound system, you wouldn't want to pull out all the stops and launch this kind of verbal attack. But if you find you're talking to a big, hostile group that's starting to take out their frustration on you, I think it's time to say a few words that puts the situation in proper perspective and gets the audience on your side.

4. Pick your anecdotes to appeal to the individuals in your audience.

One of the reasons it's important to know exactly whom you're talking to is that you'll be in a much better position to tailor your stories and statistics to the particular interests of your listeners. If you fail to keep the special identity of individual people in mind, you're likely to toss in an illustration that may at worst be offensive or at best just be irrelevant.

At the risk of seeming to fall into the fallacy of looking at groups of people as stereotypes, let me suggest a few general kinds of stories that I've found have the best chance of going over with certain audiences. If you're speaking to an all-male group and you don't know anything more about them, you're probably safe with sports anecdotes. If your audience is mostly married women who don't hold down jobs, you can probably touch a responsive chord with anecdotes about children, shopping, domestic affairs, or romance. If the group represents a mixture of sexes and individual interests, but you know it's weighted heavily in favor of married couples, then stories about marriage, marital problems, and parenthood would have the best chance of going over well. There are many joke and quip books on the market that can offer you a wide choice of illustrative and humorous material in these areas.

But these are just broad generalizations I'm making now, and I should warn you that you can't decide, "Well, Linkletter says I should tell shopping and parenthood jokes to an all-female audience, so I'll concentrate on those when I'm delivering my address to the International Feminist Population Control League." Obviously, not all female audiences, or male audiences or mixed groups, are the same, and the more specific information you can find out about exactly who the *individuals* are in the group you're addressing, the better off you'll be in selecting the appropriate stories.

For example, you may have been told you're going to be speaking to a "general audience with all sorts of interests." But a little further inquiry on your part may reveal that although the audience is indeed "general," it consists half of adults and half of children under twelve. This age mix presents the most difficult audience in the world to address, and if you start talking to them as you would the average "general" audience, you'll be lucky to get a third of the way into your speech before you lose them.

In this special situation, the sensitive speaker—and that designation now includes you, at least as far as this bit of information is concerned—knows that he must talk to the *children* and not to the grown-ups. If you can make your remarks appealing to the kids, you can assume the grown-ups will be reasonably polite because they enjoy seeing their little ones entertained. If you make the mistake of speaking only to the adults and ignore the kids, you'll lose the children almost immediately as they'll start talking and playing and complaining—and you'll end up losing the adults as well. Also, it won't work to try to go back and forth between adults and children. The attention span of a young child is so short that by the time you've spent a minute or two delivering some asides to the adults, the children will be gone from your web of influence forever.

The best way to make a talk interesting to kids, by the way, is to keep your language simple and the sentences short. Also, paint interesting word pictures with storybooklike anecdotes and illustrations. I faced a situation where I had to use this technique when I was speaking in Appleton, Wisconsin, on the subject of drugs. I was expecting an older group of students, but instead I found myself facing a large group of second graders—with a scattering of adult teachers and parents. The point I had to get across to them was that drugs are dangerous, and at first I didn't see how I could possibly put across such a sophisticated topic to such a young group.

But then I remembered the basic principle that with this many young children present, you have to talk on their level throughout the entire address. Don't fall into the trap of reverting to adult language and reasoning or you'll lose them irretrievably. So I immediately began to recast my basic drug talk in terms of going on a picnic in the mountains. After I asked them to join me in this adventure of imagination for a few minutes, I began to compare drugs to cute bears that might bite them, or lovely, peaceful streams where they might drown, or beautiful plants that could make them sick. In other words, life can be fun, but you must use caution. I put the problem of drugs in their own language and in their childish figures of speech, and I can only hope that what I said impressed them to stay away from drug abuse when they got older. But I do know that they were all riveted on my every word as we took that "hike" and "picnic" in the forests of their fantasy life.

The anecdotes you choose to tell your audience and the way you relate them should come as close as possible to resembling the way you would communicate with one or two people in a personal conversation. Obviously, the larger the group you're addressing, the harder it is to pick a set of illustrations that will appeal to everyone. But the more you can tailor those stories to the personal interests of your listeners, the easier you'll find it is to build genuine bridges of empathy and friendship with most audiences.

5. Let your listeners know you respect them.

This point may seem obvious, but you'd be surprised at the number of beginning speakers who completely ignore the accomplishments or sensitivities of their listeners. For example, if you're a salesman who has been asked to address a group of architects on some open-ended topic, you wouldn't want to insult or bore them by doing some cursory research on architecture and then attempting to tell them all about their business. Rather, you should acknowledge that they know more about architecture than you do. Then, go on to tell them what you know about salesmanship and perhaps how they can apply *your* field of expertise to improve their business and increase their number of clients.

It's also helpful to show in some small way that you're interested enough in them as individuals to have spent some time acquiring some inside information about them. For example, I was asked to speak to a convention in New York City not long ago, and I learned that in the four days the group had stayed at the hotel, there had been a number of robberies. So when I got up to speak, I said, "My speech may wander around a little this evening because while I was having a cup of coffee about an hour ago, someone stole my notes out of my room!"

This remark got a knowing laugh, and that gave me an opening to say, "Oh, has something like this happened to you too?"

The president of the group hopped up at that point and asked spontaneously, "How many of you have *not* been robbed so far?" That provided a funny lead-in to my talk, but also helped to make me a part of the group, since I had shown I understood what they had been going through.

Finally, you can let your listeners know you respect them by the courteous way you comport yourself and especially by the way you dress. The fundamental principle here is to avoid doing or wearing anything that would make you appear strangely different or dramatic. In other words, if you show up to speak to a group of staid businessmen in an open-neck sport shirt, they're going to think, "This guy doesn't know enough about the customs of the business community to realize what he should be wearing to a function like this," or they'll decide, "He doesn't care enough about our sensitivities to get dressed up for this occasion."

In most cases, it's best to wear a business suit or a similarly conservative woman's outfit no matter what group you're talking to. Even if you're giving a talk to a group of tieless laborers, you can show respect for them by dressing "up" rather than "down" when you address them. I recall a story that was told about Kenneth Strachan, the founder of the evangelistic Latin American Mission in Costa Rica. It seems that he always wore a coat and tie for his speaking engagements, even when he was delivering a talk to poor peasants who didn't even *own* a coat or tie. His reasoning was that he always wanted his listeners to know he respected them; by wearing his best clothes, he gave a concrete demonstration of this attitude.

After you've gained some experience in public speaking, you may be tempted to wear special dramatic clothes, but I'd stay away from this sort of thing. I know some professionals who wear white suits and other special costumes, but sometimes these outfits can distract from your speech. I always wear a conservative business suit myself, because I don't want my audience wondering why I have on a tie that lights up or a handkerchief that flares out. I want them to concentrate on me and what I have to say, not on any dramatic clothing.

6. Listen to your audience.

It may sound strange to advise an aspiring speaker, who is supposed to be doing the talking, to listen instead. But that's exactly what you have to do if you want to establish a good rapport with your audience.

Listening to an audience is not quite the same as listening to another person in an ordinary conversation. The way a public speaker listens is to look for nonverbal signals, such as people moving or looking around restlessly, whispering to one another, or getting up to leave before you finish. If you sense from these unspoken signals that you're losing your listeners, that's an indication that it's essential to change your pace or inject something exciting into your talk to get them with you again.

For example, you may have outlined and practiced your talk rather thoroughly, but when you actually stand up to deliver it, you discover that some of the points you're making run on too long or involve statistics or stories that aren't as interesting to the audience as you thought they would be. If this happens, be prepared to skip over some of the boring material and get into a new point or an anecdote that you suspect has a better chance of regaining their interest.

On several occasions I've run into this problem with high school kids when I'm trying to talk to them about drug abuse. I know this sort of group sometimes starts out thinking, "What does this old guy know about drugs that we don't?" and so I watch them very closely to pick up any preliminary signs of inattention, such as looking away from me or smirking or similar negative signals. One of the most effective ploys I have is to inject what I call "celebrity authority" into my talk at this point. I say something that shows I know what they're thinking about me, and yet I'm not at all threatened because I can support what I'm saying by calling on someone they know and respect.

Sometimes I'll come right out and say, "I bet a lot of you disagree with me now. You won't stand up and say so, but you're saying, 'What does he know about that?' I'll tell you what I know about it. I was with Johnny Cash at the Nashville Country Music Fair not long ago, and I said, 'Johnny, when you were on drugs, was it true that . . .'' And I'll go into some point about drug abuse I want to make. But now I've got their attention because I've piqued their interest by bringing in a singing star they respect, and I'm telling them an inside story about him. In other words, I may be making the same point I originally intended to make, but by listening to my audience and seeing that I was losing them, I backed up and explained the point from a viewpoint they understood better.

Another way is to start a nonverbal "dialogue" with your listeners. After you've determined they are drifting away from you, push them off balance with some challenge—or what I sometimes call "confrontational humor." Again, if I'm talking to a group of kids about drugs, and I can sense at the outset they're restless, I'll say, "Before I say any other thing, I want you to know I have *not* come here to tell you not to use drugs. If you want to use drugs, that's your business. Be my guest. But I am going to make a statement right now that will get a big laugh—you watch. *I know more about drugs than all of you do!*"

Then, of course, they all laugh, but I pick it right up and say, "See, I *knew* you'd take that attitude because you think I'm a square. Some of you are pushers, a lot of you are users, and most of you are out on the streets where you see this drug thing firsthand. And you're wondering what an old character from Hollywood can possibly tell you about drugs. But you wait. I'm going to tell you more about drugs than you ever thought you knew or dreamed *I* knew."

By this time, I've got them off balance and they're listening closely to what I have to say. They may be skeptical, but at least they're listening, and that's the main thing I wanted to accomplish.

An important part of establishing a friendly relationship with your audience is stressing what's commonly called "eye contact." In larger groups, though, I personally believe in looking at different segments of the audience without picking out any one person to focus on. I just keep looking around, from one group to another, and this gives people the impression that I'm looking directly at individuals. In fact, I've had many people walk up to me after a speech and tell me how much they appreciated my talking directly to them. In smaller groups, on the other hand, you may want to pick out a few individuals and look directly into their eyes, in an effort to take the "temperature" of the audience as a whole more effectively. Let me offer one word of caution here, though: Sometimes inexperienced speakers get distracted and may even forget what they're trying to say if they concentrate too hard on certain individuals. So if you find you have this problem, just glance at people briefly or at their *general* posture or body movements without looking directly into their eyes. This kind of surface interaction with your listeners should be completely adequate to inform you how well they're taking what you're trying to communicate.

Finally, every good listener in a normal one-on-one conversation makes effective use of silent spaces. In other words, he stops talking periodically and allows the other person to get a few words in. The same principle applies in a somewhat different way when you're delivering a speech, and the means you can use to take advantage of silence is the *pause*.

I often start off with a pause, just to get a group's attention. In fact, I think it's absolutely necessary that you wait for people to get quiet before you start talking, or you'll never really get their attention for the rest of the evening. If the group I'm addressing is especially noisy, I'll always say, "*Shhh*. You wouldn't want to miss anything I'm going to say, would you?" Or sometimes I'll encourage them to focus on me by suggesting, "Perhaps some of you are uncomfortable and would like to move your chairs around so that you can see me better."

The important thing is to draw their attention to you before you get started. A few preliminary, ingratiating remarks, with some pregnant pauses thrown in for effect, can do the trick.

But the pause can also be a highly effective device to keep your audience with you after you're well into your speech. I often use silent spaces when I want people to participate with me in some way—such as pondering a particularly weighty point. For example, I might say, "Let's think for a moment of all the ramifications if Proposition 13 passes [*pause*]. First of all, we might have to get by with fewer fire department services [*pause*]. Second, our police force would be cut back because you can't afford as many policemen if you don't have the same budget [*pause*]. . . ." What I would be doing here is to make each point, wait a moment or two for the point to sink in, and then move on to the next point. If the pause is too long, you risk losing the audience. But if you use just a slight hesitation, no more than a second or two, you can get a feel for whether the audience is following what you're saying with some interest. You also give them an opportunity to participate with you in a sort of unspoken dialogue.

The nervousness that often accompanies inexperience can erect a barrier between the beginning speaker and his audience, and the result may be an inability on the part of the speaker to really "hear" what his listeners are trying to tell him about his talk. But the more you speak, the more

105

sensitive you should try to become to the way your audience is reacting to you. The most powerful speakers are often not those who are so well organized or well prepared, but those who can sense the rhythm and flow of interest in an audience and then capitalize on that natural movement by well-chosen words, pauses, inflections, and gestures. It will take you some time to become adept at this sort of interaction with your listeners, but the time to get started is right now, in the very first speeches you make!

7. Maintain your personal integrity.

I've already said that it's important to respect your listeners, but there's another side of that coin. Your audience also has to show some courtesy to you, and sometimes it's up to you to straighten them out if they forget their manners. I'm not suggesting that you be heavy-handed with them—just that you make it clear, as gently as possible, that you know you have something important to say and that you have to be shown a modicum of courtesy and respect so you can do the best job of communicating.

Let me give you a few illustrations of this point. Very infrequently I've run into the problem of being flown across the country and paid up to $10,000 to deliver a forty-minute talk. But when I arrive at the place where I'm supposed to speak, the sponsor says, "Could you possibly cut it down to twenty minutes because the rest of our program has taken too long and we're running out of time?"

In a controlled, low-key tone of voice, I always reply, "No, I didn't go across this country to talk for twenty minutes. It'll take forty minutes."

106

"But that will run us over," he says.

"Well, who ran us over to begin with?" I say. "I didn't. So I'm going to talk for forty minutes."

Now you may think, "Sure, Linkletter can say something like that because he's a big-shot speaker who's getting paid $10,000. But what about me? They'll just tell me they don't want to hear me at all!"

I say, so what if they decide not to hear you? If you've been asked to deliver a half-hour talk, and somebody tells you at the last minute to cut it down to ten minutes, you're probably going to give a terrible, short little address. Very few people can make drastic last-minute changes in their material and still have it come out sounding halfway decent. So make a tough stand on your own personal integrity if anybody tries to treat you this way. You'll probably be better off not giving a speech at all than delivering a half-baked, last-minute, condensed version.

After your speech is under way, you should be prepared to meet any disruptions or big distractions head-on. I was at one big dinner in Chicago and discovered after I began talking that there was a door just to the left of the dais which people were using with great regularity to go in and out of the kitchen. At first, I thought it might be an infrequent thing, but it seemed that every time I built up to an important point, somebody would open and close that door, and half the audience would glance over to see who was entering or leaving.

Finally, I stopped and said, "I have now arrived at the most important part of my speech because what's at stake is whether or not I continue. I want somebody to go over and stand next to that door and prevent anyone else from going in or out. I don't know what's in there—if it's a men's room, then they're in there for the rest of the speech. But I can't go on watching you watch that door for the next thirty minutes."

Now, this may seem a stronger statement than what you would want to say to one of your audiences. But I think *something* has to be said, or your entire speech will be ruined. And if you make your protest in the right way, with a light tone of voice, you may well get a laugh—in addition to getting some respect from your listeners.

A related disruption might involve a crying baby. I usually put up with a couple of loud cries or shouts. But after that, I say in a kind but serious voice, "I wonder if the mother of that child would mind taking him out so we can all get something out of this talk?" I get bothered by this sort of interruption because I know the audience is bothered, and the care and feeding of an audience is my most important concern when I'm up in front of them. I don't want them to be too hot or too cold. I want them to be able to hear me. And I want every possible distraction removed so that they can focus on everything I have to say. It's hard enough to give an outstanding speech when all the conditions are perfect, so the more obstacles you can get rid of, the better.

8. Take good care of yourself before each speech.

A speech is in some respects a lot like an athletic event. To do your best, you should prepare yourself physically—not necessarily by doing exercises (though I find my energy level and stamina increase when I'm in good shape) but certainly by getting plenty of rest. *Remember*: No matter how experienced you are, you'll always feel some tension before you deliver a talk, and if you're fatigued to begin with, you could find yourself running out of steam in the middle of the speech.

So get plenty of sleep the night before, relax by lying down or napping if possible sometime during the day of the speech, and stay away from lengthy cocktail parties just before your talk. I'm often asked to attend cocktail parties before one of my talks, but I always say quite honestly, "I don't drink, but I'll tell you what I'll do. You get together the people who want to meet me at the cocktail party about fifteen minutes before it's scheduled to end. Then I'll come over there and shake their hands, and I'll go right from there to give my speech."

In this way, I don't offend anybody by not showing up at all, but at the same time I don't wear myself out for an hour or more standing around and talking just before I'm supposed to get up and talk for another hour.

And this stress on keeping physically fit and rested just stands to reason, doesn't it? After all, if you're getting together for a small party in the evening, you don't feel much like casual conversation if you're exhausted from your activities earlier in the day. The same basic principle applies to giving a talk to an audience—except that the physical tension and demands on your ability to perform and be interesting are much greater than in a group of your personal friends. When you accept an invitation to speak to a group, you assume a heavy responsibility to do the best job you can and to communicate with them as effectively as possible. There's no way you can do your best if you allow yourself to get run down before you even step up to the podium.

In some ways, I consider this chapter to be the most important section in the book. If you can establish a good rapport with your audience—if you can make them like you and root for you as you deliver your address—you'll probably achieve more than you will if you're merely a technically adept, well-prepared speaker. The key element in most good speeches is your ability to project the image that you're a friendly person whose primary aim is to help your listeners in some important way. Good speaking is largely a matter of good personal relations, so always focus first on making friends with your audience. Charm them before you try to convince or convert them!

CHAPTER EIGHT

☙ ☙ ☙

The Art of Persuasion

W e've already seen—even though you may not really believe it yet—that your audience is more than likely to be favorably disposed or at least neutral toward you.

But what if you run into an unfriendly or skeptical audience? What if you can't count on their taking everything you say at face value, but instead you have to convince or persuade them of your point of view?

At the prospect of confronting a hostile group of listeners, many inexperienced speakers are tempted to run in the opposite direction rather than take a chance on being rejected or hooted down in public. There's really no reason to take such a negative attitude. If you can just get off on the right foot with an audience like this and lead them gently along in the direction you want them to go, they can present you with almost as easy a speaking assignment as a group that's completely sympathetic to your viewpoint.

Here's a helpful procedure I've come up with after speaking to many groups who were at best lukewarm to my topic, and at worst actively hostile:

Begin with a point of agreement.

There's always *something* you and your listeners can agree on—even if it's only the fact that you're from the same state or you're in favor of small children, dogs, and apple pie. Ease into your speech with an assertion that you are all in harmony on some point and then move into your substantive remarks from that beginning. Avoid controversial topics or issues like the plague when you first start out in a speech. If you hit them immediately with something you know they don't like, you're asking for trouble—and an ineffective speech.

Move ahead with your speech by discussing topics from their viewpoint.

In other words, you've already managed to get in tune with them by bringing up something you agree on. Now don't blow it by in effect saying, "We may agree on that first point I made, but we're certainly at odds on everything else!" Keep the orientation of your audience in mind throughout the speech and organize the topics you want to discuss by hitting them first with the least objectionable thing, then the next least objectionable, and so on.

✓ **Lead them in short steps to the conclusion you want them to reach.**

If you move them too quickly toward the position you want to persuade them is right, you're likely to lose them before you get there. Think very seriously about each step in your speech that is leading them to the final conclusion. At what point or points are you most likely to find them drawing back and saying, "Now just a darned minute—I can go along with what he's said up to now, but this is where I draw the line"? Don't allow them to draw any lines! If you find a point where you think you're likely to lose them, rework that part of your speech so that it's more convincing, or so that it leads them in shorter steps—rather than one big leap—to the next affirmation you want them to make.

To illustrate these three elements in an effective speech of persuasion, let me give you a couple of illustrations from my own experience and then we'll take a look at a couple of well-known historical examples. I recently spoke before the Wisconsin Board of Educators in Milwaukee about the problems of teaching children, and I knew when I accepted the invitation that I would have several things going for me and several things against me. First, I knew that the audience would probably be curious to hear me speak merely because most of them would have seen me on television; they had read about my being the father of five children; and also they would know I had many years of experience in interviewing children. At the same time, they would think that I had no experience as a teacher and might be skeptical about my credentials to talk to them about kids in a classroom.

So when I stood up before them, I presented my talk in the format of persuasion I've just described to you. I said, "I feel almost like one of you because I'm on the Board of Trustees of Springfield College and of the Art Center College of Design. Also, though you may not know it, I studied to be a schoolteacher and have a B.A. degree. I might well have been an underpaid teacher who would now be here to ask you for a big raise if I hadn't happened to get into a business that brought me a slightly larger classroom than some of your teachers have. My classroom—and that's the way I look at it—has been 55 billion people over radio and television airwaves in the past forty years, instead of a few thousand restless kids. But I don't think my problems have been more challenging than the ones you face."

What I've done here is to associate myself right away with the field of education by identifying myself as a student of teaching who is still very interested in the field of education.

Then I take another small step of leading them into my topic of the problems of children in the classroom by saying, "Most of you are parents, and some of you are old enough to have teenagers or older children, as I do. Anyone who has wrestled with the problems of adolescents must agree with what Mark Twain said when he remarked that he loved children, but when they're thirteen they should be put into a barrel and fed through a bunghole until they are sixteen, at which time the bunghole should be permanently sealed up."

This invariably gets a big laugh because we're all suddenly looking at the problems of raising teenagers, from the same viewpoint. After this, it became easy to persuade them of the points I wanted to make about the best way to deal with kids in a classroom because they finally accepted the premise that I really knew something about their practical problems as educators.

On another occasion, I was asked to speak on drug abuse in Ponca City, Oklahoma, and I immediately wondered, "How on earth am I going to convince the people in that little southwestern town that they have a drug problem like everybody else? And how likely are they going to be to listen to what some outside big-city slicker has to say about the topic?"

Once again, I fell back on my simple procedure for persuasion. I said right at the beginning of my talk, "Back in Hollywood, people asked me where I was going this weekend, and I said, 'Ponca City.' They said, 'What are you going to a little town like that for?' I said, 'What do you mean a little town? I was born in Moose Jaw, Saskatchewan—a town where they had to widen the main street so they could paint a yellow stripe down the middle! A town where the welcome and goodbye were painted on the same sign! A town where the kids used to get together on Saturday nights and watch somebody get shaved!

"I know a little town like this isn't well-known, but it's little towns like this that really make America what it is today. You people live together in families, and those small units in our society are what make our nation great. The United States is not New York, Chicago, San Francisco, or Los Angeles. It's hundreds and hundreds of Ponca Cities!"

The audience loved this, and I wasn't kidding them either. I believe what I was saying is true. But the important point for our purposes was that I picked something we could agree on at the outset of my talk, then the challenge was to keep them agreeing with me as I moved forward with my presentation. I wanted them to be absolutely clear I didn't regard myself as some big shot who had come to town to look down my nose at them.

So I continued, "You're farmers, and so am I. I didn't know what a farmer's life was until I bought a farm in

Australia a number of years ago. But I learned quickly. I found I was at the mercy of the rain, wind, and prices. And no matter how hard you work, somebody in some obscure government position can pull the plug on you."

After establishing the fact that I identified with them, that we agreed on a number of things, and that I respected them for being fine representatives of our country, I launched out onto the more dangerous waters of my main theme—how the drug problem in America relates to Ponca City. "Unfortunately," I said, "whether you believe it or not, just as you are part of the warp and woof of America, so you are subject to the same ills as the rest of the country. You may not have the same sensational drug problems, like heroin and cocaine, but you have drinking and you have pills. I don't have to come in here and ask what your drug problem is because I already know. The problem you're facing is spread all across America, in every stratum of our society. We have been conditioned to think that we are entitled to be happy all the time. If you're not happy, you may swallow, snort, sniff, or inject some substance that's illegal. Or you may take something that's legal, but still potentially dangerous, like Valium."

My main purpose in shaping a speech like this is to get a strong reaction of agreement from the audience and then build a sort of *momentum* of affirmative vibrations between myself and my listeners. It's always important to identify with your audience in every talk, as we've seen in earlier chapters. But in a speech of persuasion, the positive vibrations between you and your listeners become doubly imperative because if you lose them in your early remarks, you'll never hold them—and convince them—as you move into the tougher, more controversial sections of your talk. The momentum of agreement you establish in your first

116

few words should carry you over to the body of your speech on a wave of enthusiasm and affirmation.

The more hostile your audience, the more important it is to establish this firm foundation of agreement right at the beginning of your talk. I've mentioned some initially negative reactions I've received from young audiences when I stand up to talk to them about drugs. But like any other hostile group, they can respond as favorably to this "art of persuasion" I'm describing as to any other speech-making ploy.

When I stood up to speak to one obviously hostile high school group, I decided to try to establish a bond of agreement between myself and the kids by saying, "I can see that some of you here feel I'm going to lecture you sternly about the use of drugs—but that's not the case. I want to talk about drugs because they just fascinate me. Let's take aspirin for example—a wonderful drug that can do wonderful things. But it might surprise you to know that when it's abused by overuse, it's one of the most dangerous drugs in the United States. I'm not interested in talking only about things that make you high but about the sensible use of *anything* you put into your body. If you take too much aspirin too often, for instance, you can cause abdominal hemorrhaging.

"I'm not here to point the finger only at you kids about popping angel dust or pills or acid. We're all guilty of drug abuse. Believe it or not, seventy percent of all overdose problems in the United States today involve women thirty-five to forty-five years of age. That means, for some of you, your mothers and grandmothers. And why do they do this? Because inexperienced doctors have convinced them they are nervous and upset and should swallow some Valium or Librium. They get hooked as surely as if they were on heroin."

Up to this point, I've been saying things that I hope all the kids in the audience can agree with. Also, I'm not pointing the finger directly at them. In fact, I'm pointing *away* from them, to the very adults who may be accusing them of being potheads.

And I *continue* to point away from them as I move ahead in my speech, but now I also begin to look for an opportunity to drive home to them my point about problems they may be facing as well. "What do you think is the worst drug in the entire United States? It's liquor, booze. And the worst offenders with liquor are adults—again, maybe your parents and grandparents. What these adults are doing may at first glance seem to be fun, exciting, even mature. I remember when I was a kid, I tried sneaking out behind the garage to smoke a cigarette, partly because I had seen adults doing it and it seemed exciting. But the difference today is that if you decide to sneak out behind the garage and pop some of the pills and other drugs that are available, you are taking a risk of ruining your entire life. Let me show you what I mean. . . ."

There's a strong probability that if I start off a speech this way to a group of skeptical kids, with solid areas of agreement being established between us, they'll at least continue to listen for a while as I move into that segment of my talk that relates directly to them. I've persuaded them, in other words, that I'm worth listening to and that we have enough in common to give me some standing to speak authoritatively to them.

But I don't want to give you the impression that I think I'm the first person to come up with this approach to persuading an audience. One of the classic models of an effective speech of persuasion was formulated several hundred years ago by William Shakespeare in his *Julius Caesar*. Let's take a few moments to analyze that speech and see what the old Bard has to say to us about the proper way to convince an audience.

In act 3, scene 2, we find Caesar dead, having been murdered by Brutus and a group of conspirators. Brutus has openly confessed to the Romans that he killed Caesar because of the ruler's excessive ambition, and the crowd is shouting their approval of the deed with such cries as "Live, Brutus! live, live!" "Bring him with triumph home unto his house," and "Let him be Caesar."

Then Brutus departs and Mark Antony arrives to speak to the crowd *against* Brutus, but they're not as sympathetic to him as they were to Brutus. They mutter, " 'Twere best he speak no harm of Brutus here," "This Caesar was a tyrant," and "We are bless'd that Rome is rid of him."

So Antony, a friend of Caesar and an enemy of Brutus, has his work cut out for him if he hopes to swing this opinionated, partisan crowd to his side. To accomplish his purpose, he immediately launches into a classic speech of persuasion. Let's analyze it from start to finish to see how Antony's technique compares with the method we've been discussing.

"Friends, Romans, countrymen, lend me your ears; I come to bury Caesar, not to praise him. The evil that men do lives after them, the good is oft interred with their bones; so let it be with Caesar."

You can see that Antony immediately establishes a point of agreement with his audience. He stresses that the people in the audience are his friends and fellow citizens. They both come from the same background and have similar national goals. Also, he starts out in a rather negative vein as far as Caesar is concerned—and by those remarks is demonstrating to the crowd that his attitude toward Caesar is in harmony with theirs.

He goes on, "The noble Brutus hath told you Caesar

was ambitious: If it were so, it was a grievous fault, and grievously hath Caesar answer'd it. Here, under leave of Brutus and the rest—for Brutus is an honourable man; so are they all honourable men—come I to speak in Caesar's funeral."

Here we have some highly subtle argument. Antony states Brutus' accusations against Caesar without actually agreeing with them. He acknowledges that "if it were so" that Caesar was ambitious, then it was a serious fault. But he doesn't say he himself believes that Caesar was ambitious. Still, the way he expresses himself allows him to keep the audience on his side without telling them an outright lie about the way he feels. Also, Antony introduces Brutus and the other killers into this speech in such a way that the crowd will agree with his reference to them. We may know there's an element of sarcasm or at least irony in his description of them as "honourable," but the crowd will just continue to nod at his words because they don't suspect at this point the ultimate destination to which he's leading them.

Antony continues, "He [Caesar] was my friend, faithful and just to me: But Brutus says he was ambitious; and Brutus is an honourable man. He hath brought many captives home to Rome, whose ransoms did the general coffers fill: Did this in Caesar seem ambitious?"

Now Antony, having pulled the crowd solidly over to his side with several points of agreement, begins to turn his talk gradually in a different direction. First, he offers a personal observation—that Caesar was his friend and had always been good to him. His listeners might believe that Caesar was a bad guy in *general* terms, but they would be unlikely to accuse Antony of lying about his own specific relationship with the ruler. He also restates Brutus' accusations about Caesar being ambitious—apparently in an effort to balance out his own positive remark. Citing your opponents' points is a good ploy in any effective argument because this approach at least gives the impression that you're bending over backward to be fair: You're presenting the bad with the good and not attempting to hide anything.

This tactic has also been called "stealing the thunder" of the opposite point of view. Your audience has probably made up its mind because of one or two key ideas that have been planted by those representing the opposing viewpoint. In this case, Brutus has riled them up with arguments about Caesar's overbearing ambition. Instead of ignoring this point as though it didn't exist, Antony pulls the accusation right out into the open and acknowledges Brutus' justification for holding such a viewpoint (i.e., he's "honourable"), but he then goes on to poke a few holes in this negative attitude toward Caesar.

After easing into his main argument with a personal comment about Caesar, Antony begins to stress the inconsistencies in Brutus' position with some hard-hitting, concrete evidence. His first point is that Caesar conquered Rome's enemies and put the booty he acquired into the Roman treasury, not into his own pocket. But he doesn't try to impose his own interpretation of this fact directly on his listeners. Instead, he lets them come to their own conclusions by asking whether they consider such actions by Caesar ambitious.

Antony then continues with a similar line of argument: "When that the poor have cried, Caesar hath wept: Ambition should be made of sterner stuff: Yet Brutus says he was ambitious; and Brutus is an honourable man. You all did see that on the Lupercal I thrice presented him a kingly crown, which he did thrice refuse: Was this ambition? Yet Brutus says he was ambitious; and, sure, he is an honourable man. I speak not to disprove what Brutus spoke, but here I am to speak what I do know. You all did love him once, not without cause: What cause withholds you then to mourn for him? O judgment! thou art fled to brutish beasts, and men have lost their reason. Bear with me; my heart is in the coffin there with Caesar, and I must pause till it come back to me."

Now we've reached the crux of the matter. Antony hits them hard with fact after fact, and then reaches an emotional conclusion, indicating that he considers the evidence overwhelmingly in favor of Caesar's goodness—even though Brutus and the conspirators are "honourable men."

Antony's audience has already swung toward his way of thinking. Listen to what some of them say:

"Methinks there is much reason in his sayings."

"If thou consider rightly of the matter, Caesar has had great wrong."

"Poor soul! His eyes are red as fire with weeping."

"There's not a nobler man in Rome than Antony."

Now that Antony has the momentum of the crowd's emotions and reason moving in his direction, he brings out his heavy forensic artillery. He reveals that Caesar has left a last will and testament, and the crowd goes into a near frenzy in their eagerness to hear what it says.

But Antony keeps them straining at the bit for a moment longer. "Have patience, gentle friends; I must not read it: It is not meet you know how Caesar loved you. You are not wood, you are not stones, but men; and, being men, hearing the will of Caesar, it will inflame you, it will make you mad. 'Tis good you know not that you are his heirs; for if you should, O! what would come of it!"

I always chuckle when I read this passage because Antony is once again bolstering his argument with material he knows his audience will agree with. But this time, he's not appealing to their reason or their inclination to be friendly with him, but rather to their pocketbooks. The lesson for you here is that if you can show your audience how the conclusion you want them to reach can improve them financially (or in any other personal way, for that matter), you'll go a long way toward persuading them of your viewpoint.

The response of the crowd is predictable. They now go all the way to Antony's position in opposing Brutus and the conspirators, as they shout, "They were traitors . . . villains . . . murderers. The will! read the will."

Antony's speech is one of the most famous in all literature, and I believe one of the main reasons it has had such an impact over the years is that it touches a responsive chord in those who read it or hear it performed. We *know* we're listening to a powerful speech of persuasion, and we enjoy being convinced anew of the justice of Antony's position—and the wrongness and guilt of Brutus'. I would encourage you to pull out that dusty volume of Shakespeare on your library shelf and read over this entire passage again, with the detailed reactions of Antony's listeners. I've spent a fair amount of time describing this passage, but there's more, much more, in the original.

Before we leave our consideration of the art of persuading an audience, I'd like to invite you to take another historical journey with me—this time only about a hundred years into the past—to a real speech and a real crowd at a political rally in our own country. I'm referring to the famous "Cross of Gold" address delivered by the incomparable turn-of-the-century orator, William Jennings Bryan.

Bryan was only thirty-six years old when he arrived at the Democratic National Convention in Chicago in 1896.

The Democratic party, though the party in power under President Cleveland, was in disarray because the country had just gone through three years of depression—and the incumbent was regarded as responsible.

In an effort to come up with a solution to the nation's economic problems and thereby retrieve the fortunes of the Democrats, the leaders at the convention locked horns on one major issue—whether the gold standard should be the exclusive standard for American money, or whether silver should also be used. The delegates tended to polarize around these two metals, with the business interests of the East flocking to gold and the agrarian groups in the West and South embracing silver.

The "silverites" seemed to have a lot going for them, with plenty of enthusiasm and votes. But they lacked a leader. That's where William Jennings Bryan, with his tremendous powers of persuasion, was made to order. Despite his youth, Bryan was known to be a man of great intellect, character, and conviction, and so he automatically commanded a hearing even if his listeners were inclined to disagree with him. His chance to demonstrate his ability to convince others came during the debate on the gold standard during the formulation of the party platform. The prior speeches hadn't satisfied the silver forces, and many were beginning to wonder if the right balance could be struck in stating the position of the silverites forcefully and effectively.

Bryan's persuasiveness began to exert itself in the very way he was dressed as he strode to the speaker's platform. He was wearing a typical, unadorned westerner's outfit with baggy pants, vest, and black suit. And he began his talk in a way that no one—not even the staunchest proponents of the gold standard—could find fault:

"It would be presumptuous indeed, to present myself against the distinguished gentlemen to whom you have listened, if this were a mere measuring of abilities; but this is not a contest between persons. The humblest citizen in all the land, when clad in the armor of a righteous cause, is stronger than all the hosts of error. I come to speak to you in defense of a cause as holy as the cause of liberty—the cause of humanity."

At this point, he's for humanity, not silver, and everybody can agree with that. As we've seen before, you try to get everybody to agree with you at first and then nurse them along, maintaining that momentum of agreement so that when you reach your ultimate point, you still have as many following you as possible.

Bryan stressed over and over in the first part of his speech that he regarded the gold-silver debate as impersonal. He didn't want to bring it down to the level of mudslinging between personalities. By taking the high road in this way, he was able to couch his argument in terms of lofty principles and not debased prejudice and bias. And the audience embraced him from the outset. They began to interrupt him regularly with applause and shouts so that he started thinking of them almost as a "trained choir."*

But not everybody was with him, even at this point. One farmer who was listening to the oratory was heard to say, "I think I'll go because I do not care to stay to hear that crazy Populist, Bill Bryan of Nebrasky." But just as the man was about to depart, Bryan touched a "hot spot" of agreement with him in this creative definition of who constituted a valid businessman:

---

* For a detailed description of the impact of the speech, see Paolo E. Coletta, *William Jennings Bryan: I, Political Evangelist, 1860-1908* (Lincoln, Neb.: University of Nebraska Press, 1964), pp. 137–49.

"The man who is employed for wages is as much a business man as his employer; the attorney in a country town is as much a business man as the corporation counsel in a great metropolis; the merchant at the crossroads store is as much a business man as the merchant of New York; *the farmer who goes forth in the morning and toils all day*—who begins in the spring and toils all summer—and who by the application of brain and muscle to the natural resources of the country creates wealth, is as much a business man as the man who goes upon the board of trade and bets upon the price of grain; the miners who go down a thousand feet into the earth, or climb two thousand feet upon the cliffs, and bring forth from their hiding places the precious metals to be poured into the channels of trade, are as much business men as the few financial magnates who in a back room, corner the money of the world. We come to speak for this broader class of business men."

The critical farmer, upon hearing that Bryan had included his occupation in this definition, threw his hat into the air, beat on the seat in front of him, and shouted, "God! My God! My God!" And he was joined in another wave of shouts when the speaker mentioned "miners."

Bryan, in other words, pulled as many of the divergent interest groups in the audience as possible together under one umbrella of agreement before he stressed the controversial core of his argument—the problem of the gold standard. He continued to stress his affirmation of those political principles he knew his listeners also believed in, and gradually, under this cloak of harmony, he eased into the gold issue. Finally, he reached the climax of his argument in his peroration, the concluding section of his speech for which he has become famous. Let's take a look at it to see how far he had been able to lead his divided audience through his powers of persuasion:

126

"You [referring to the gold standard advocates] come to us and tell us that the great cities are in favor of the gold standard; we reply that the great cities rest upon our broad and fertile prairies. Burn down your cities and leave our farms, and your cities will spring up again as if by magic; but destroy our farms and the grass will grow in the streets of every city in the country.

"My friends, we declare that this nation is able to legislate for its own people upon every question, without waiting for the aid or consent of any other nation on earth; and upon that issue we expect to carry every state in the Union. I shall not slander the inhabitants of the fair State of Massachusetts nor the inhabitants of the State of New York by saying that, when they are confronted with the proposition, they will declare that this nation is not able to attend to its own business. It is the issue of 1776 over again. Our ancestors, when but three millions in number, had the courage to declare their political independence of every other nation; shall we, their descendants, when we have grown to seventy millions, declare that we are less independent than our forefathers? No, my friends, that will never be the verdict of our people. Therefore, we care not upon what lines the battle is fought. If they say bimetallism is good, but that we cannot have it until other nations help us, we reply that, instead of having a gold standard because England has, we will restore bimetallism, and then let England have bimetallism because the United States has it. If they dare to come out in the open field and defend the gold standard as a good thing, we will fight then to the uttermost. Having behind us the producing masses of this nation and the world, supported by the commercial interests, the laboring interests, and the toilers everywhere, we will answer their demand for a gold standard by saying to them: You shall not press down upon the brow of labor this crown of thorns, you shall not crucify mankind upon a cross of gold!"

Bryan punctuated the last sentence of his speech with a couple of dramatic gestures. First, as he said "crown of thorns," he clawed at his head with his fingers, as though he were being ripped by a crown of thorns himself. And then, as he uttered "cross of gold," he swung both his arms out wide to his sides, and stood in this position for several seconds, a dramatic representation of man crucified before the crowd's very eyes.

So powerful was the impact of his closing that the audience remained in dead silence until he started walking toward his seat—and then an earthshaking uproar welled up from all parts of the floor. The result of the speech was that the "silverites," or bimetallists, won the party platform fight, and Bryan was chosen as the Democratic nominee for President in 1896. He eventually lost the election, but the campaign—which had been kicked off by his great "Cross of Gold" speech—thrust him into national prominence and helped ensure him a permanent place in the pantheon of American history makers.

Now I'm not suggesting that you should aspire to become another William Jennings Bryan or Mark Antony, but I think their classic speeches of persuasion can be highly instructive for the amateur as well as the professional. As I mentioned in Chapter Four on the basic ingredients of a speech, *every* good speech should have a few introductory words that enable the speaker to identify with the audience. But in a speech of persuasion, the *momentum of agreement*, which must start building from the very first words out of your mouth, is the central organizing principle. If necessary, you should place more controversial sections farther back in your speech, even if they would seem to fit more logically nearer the beginning. A symmetrically arranged speech means nothing if you alienate your audience at the outset. To persuade most effectively, then, think in terms of moving gradually from one point of agreement to another until you can shift quite naturally—and agreeably—into the main point you want to make.

But words are not the only means of persuasion or of getting your point across in any sort of speech you make. Many speakers make effective use of physical props to demonstrate what they are trying to say, and that's the next topic I want to discuss with you.

CHAPTER NINE

☙ ☙ ☙

The Prop Principle

O ne of your main objectives as a speaker should be to leave your listeners with an indelible impression of the major points in your speech. Often, it should be possible to achieve this goal just by your verbal virtuosity. But sometimes you may feel you need a little help, and that's where the "prop principle" comes into play.

A prop is nothing more than a physical object (or even a person) that helps you get your audience's attention and illustrates your main theme more effectively. For example, I remember years ago I saw one guy give a speech on salesmanship. He said, "If you're going to sell effectively, you have to get the buyer's attention." Then he suddenly

131

reached into his back pocket, pulled out a pistol, and fired it into the air. The audience, of course, was shocked so badly they didn't dare take their eyes off him.

"Now that was an extreme example," he said as he put the pistol back in his pocket. "I certainly wouldn't suggest that you fire a gun in a person's office to get his attention. But the pistol illustrates what I'm getting at—one way or another, you must keep those buyers listening closely to you!"

As a result of this speaker's prop, I doubt that audience *ever* forgot his main point. But just to make sure, he occasionally reached back toward the pistol again and asked, "You remember the most important lesson in this talk, don't you?" They laughed, but it was clear they got the point.

I don't use props myself, but a lot of good speakers do. They feel that if you show an audience a physical object, the very act of viewing the object reinforces the point you're making with your words. Public speaking instructors in the U.S. military and in various business speaking courses emphasize this principle. They encourage speakers to state their case verbally and then, through the use of charts, graphs, slides, and other physical means, to restate their major themes in another way. The main idea is that the more you hear or see something in a variety of ways, the more likely you are to understand and remember it.

I recall one speaker who was talking about the "Ten Steps to Success," and to illustrate his concept he dragged out a stepladder. As he described the first step to success, he mounted the first rung of the ladder. Speaking to his audience from this elevated position, he declared, "Hard work is the first step you have to take if you're going to succeed. You're never going to get anywhere if you don't work hard!"

Then when he moved on to his second point—the importance of education in success—he stepped up to the second rung. By the time he reached his final point, he was sitting precariously on the top of the ladder, gazing down over his listeners as they craned their necks up to follow what he was saying.

"Now you're sitting on top of the world because you've taken all the steps you need to be a big success in life," he said.

I'll admit this seemed a little corny to me—but I still remember the main thrust of his talk, even though I've completely forgotten thousands of other speeches I've heard over the years. So I would suggest that you at least evaluate each talk you plan to give in light of these three basic tests, to see if the prop principle might apply:

1. Is it *possible* to use a prop naturally in my speech, without straining to include it?
2. Even if it's possible, is it *appropriate* to use a prop, or would a physical object actually detract from the speech because of the peculiar setting of the speech?
3. If it's possible and appropriate, *which prop or props* would help me make the greatest impact on my audience?

Now let me explain each of these points in somewhat greater detail. You might decide after looking over your speech on overseas bribery in international corporations, that there just aren't any points, statistics, or other elements in your talk that lend themselves to physical demonstration. If so, discard the idea of using props immediately. A graph, chart, physical object, or other prop that doesn't quite fit into a talk will have the same negative impact as an irrelevant anecdote or statistic. Your audience will begin to question whether you're really well organized and well prepared on your subject.

On the other hand, you may find that a physical object would illustrate a section of your talk quite well, but for some reason it might be better to avoid the use of props altogether. Suppose, for instance, that you've been asked by your pastor to give the yearly lay sermon at your church. One of the points you want to make is that there is a connection between a person's treatment of dumb animals and his treatment of human beings. Your text might be Proverbs 12:10, which in the New English Bible reads, "A righteous man cares for his beast, but a wicked man is cruel at heart." Now, it might be quite possible and even highly relevant to discuss how both humans and animals respond positively to kind treatment—but that doesn't mean it would be appropriate to bring a live horse or dog into the pulpit to demonstrate the point.

Finally, if you determine that one or more props could help you give a better speech, you have to select the ones that will have the greatest impact. As you make this choice, I would suggest you keep a couple of things in mind. First of all, limit the number of props you use to as few as possible. If only one will accomplish your purpose, then stick to that one. The speaker with the pistol in our earlier example wanted to stress the importance of getting a buyer's attention, and the audience tended to associate his main point with his single prop. He was the "man with the pistol" to his listeners, and I doubt any of them forgot his central theme after they went home. If you have a half dozen objects, charts, or other objects, they'll probably merge with one another and lose their effectiveness.

Second, when you're choosing props, pick them in order of descending importance. Also, if possible, always use at least one of them to illustrate your major or dominant theme. The first one you choose should thus illustrate your most important point, the next your second most important point, and so on. This way, if you limit yourself to just two or three props, you'll be certain that they will at least reinforce your key themes and not some minor ideas that are peripheral to the main thrust of your speech.

As a matter of fact, I believe it's usually best to stick to only one prop per speech, provided it illustrates your central theme. John Wooden, former basketball coach of UCLA, is doing consulting work and inspirational speaking these days, and one of his most popular talks deals with what he calls the "pyramid of success." To illustrate this theme he uses one prop—a large model of a pyramid, with personal qualities like "perseverance," "enthusiasm," and "sincerity" indicated at each level. Then, like the fellow we saw earlier with the stepladder but in a much more dignified manner, Wooden builds his entire speech around the construction of the pyramid. This single prop acts as an effective visual aid and memory device and reinforces the main theme of his talk.

Sometimes, props can be used as much to entertain an audience as to instruct them or aid their memory. I recall one talk I heard on salesmanship where the speaker had a beautiful model walk behind him periodically as he spoke. Each time she would stroll by, she'd have fewer clothes on until finally, when she was down to a brief bikini, the speaker turned around, pointed to her, and said, "The final point I want to make is that you have to do a good job of displaying your product!"

An even more frivolous example of this sort of thing was a vaudeville technique used by the old stage entertainer known as "Professor Lamberti." He would come out in an oversized suit, with hair brushed up on each end and baggy pants flopping about, and would get ready to play on a xylophone. As he finished the first short chorus, a stripper would walk out on the stage behind him and remove one article of clothing before going offstage. The applause would be deafening, so he'd bow and do another chorus. This was repeated until she slipped out of her bra and made a quick exit. When the audience had finally quieted down, he would smile happily and say, "I'm glad you like my music."

The use of real people as "props" may not appeal to you. But the point I want to make is that if you're inclined to use props, you should at least consider using real people as well as inanimate objects. A talk on "dressing for success" in a corporate job, for example, might be effectively—*and* tastefully—demonstrated by the use of live men and women who are wearing the kinds of clothes that illustrate your major points.

As I mentioned earlier, I'm not really inclined to use props at all because I prefer to have every eye focused on me and on what I'm saying. I value eye contact and personal interaction with my audience so highly that I don't want to take a chance on having anything get in the way of that relationship. But many effective speakers take the opposite viewpoint. My friend Ira Hayes, who calls himself the "ambassador of enthusiasm," does a great job using all sorts of props at positive-thinking rallies around the country. He employs cardboard figures, dumbbells, and other such devices to demonstrate how you can "exercise" your mind as well as your body.

In the last analysis, the decision to use props is mostly a matter of personal style. If you feel awkward holding up a cardboard figure or climbing a stepladder, your discomfort is going to show, and your speech will suffer. But if a prop seems to fit naturally into a particular talk, feel free to use it.

In any case, it's always good to know how to handle a physical object in front of any audience because sometimes you really have no choice. I'll get into some mandatory or near-mandatory uses of graphs, charts, and slides later when we discuss giving a business presentation. But there's an even more common kind of prop that you may find you have to use—even though you may not want to—and that's the set of notes or script for your speech.

Actually, many people don't think of notes as a prop in a speech, but they are. Any physical object you're holding or referring to, which tends to attract your audience's eye, is a "prop" in the most accurate sense of the term. The problem with notes is that in the view of both the speaker and the audience, they more often than not have a negative rather than positive effect on the total impact of a speech. But this doesn't have to be so. This subject is so important and far-reaching that I've decided to devote the entire next chapter to it.

CHAPTER TEN

⚓ ⚓ ⚓

The Great Notes Debate

One of the main reasons people are afraid of public speaking is that they fear their minds will go blank when they stand up before an audience.

For beginning speakers, this is a reasonable fear. It is easy to get rattled and forget your next point if you're inexperienced and have a group of strangers staring at you, hanging on your every word. This problem has several solutions, one of the most effective of which is learning to speak smoothly from notes.

Some purists believe it's always bad to speak from notes because they can get in the way of intimate interaction between you and your listeners. This is the

139

essence of what I call "the great notes debate." In other words, are notes by nature an impediment to good public speaking, which you should eventually try to avoid at all costs as you become more experienced? Or should you incorporate the use of notes as a basic, continuing part of your public speaking skills?

There is some truth in the criticisms of notes, especially if you don't know the best ways to use them. But with a little training—which I'm about to give you—and a little practice, you should find that notes can give you confidence without getting in the way of the friendship you want to establish with your audience.

Even if you consider yourself a good natural speaker who really doesn't need notes, I would strongly advise you at least to learn how to speak from them effectively. The reason? No matter how articulate you are or how good your memory is, you're bound to face a speaking situation at some point in which you'd feel more comfortable with notes. Perhaps your topic is unusually complex, your setting particularly distracting, or the subject matter sufficiently important that you have to be absolutely accurate. If you find yourself in this kind of speaking assignment but without the requisite skills at using notes smoothly, you may be in trouble from the moment you open your mouth.

My first major point about the effective use of notes is one I've already touched on elsewhere in this book: If you use notes, don't try to hide them! Put them or hold them right out in plain view (unless you have a podium) and feel free to refer to them as you speak. They can become as natural a prop for your speech as the stepladders and pistols we discussed in the previous chapter.

For example, you might say near the beginning of your speech, "I've jotted down three main things that I think we have to be concerned about in evaluating the future of this town. Now let's consider each of them in turn: First, the automobile production will drop off from now on, and let me take a moment to explain how this is going to happen. . . . The second point I've written down here is that the coal we've been using to keep our factory generators running is going to be diverted to other parts of the country, and we have to find some new sources of energy. . . . The third point is that you can expect to face some big problems with our tourists in the future. You might ask why we should have problems with tourists in the future since we haven't even seen a tourist in the past few years. The answer is that as you know, we've just discovered a local version of Carlsbad Caverns, and tourists are already lining up trips to see them. But what you *don't* know is that there is a seepage of poisonous gas in those caverns, which will not only kill all our tourists but will most likely render the entire town uninhabitable!"

As you're referring to each of your major points in this speech, you might actually wave your notes before your audience or point your finger at the papers when you say, "The second point I've written down here." This open use of your notes will put your audience at ease and help them accept your holding notes or looking down at them as a completely natural part of your presentation. Also, just as with any other prop, calling their attention to your notes when you make an important point may well reinforce that point in their minds. They may think, "Since he's moving to the next key item on that list of his, I'd better try especially hard to remember what it is."

In addition to learning to use notes openly as props, it's also important to develop a speaking style with them that is completely natural and conversational. The person who doesn't know the proper way to use notes will probably seem stiff and halting as he tries to deliver his speech. It's this lack of skill in using notes that has led many experienced speakers to advise beginners to learn to speak without any written references from the outset. I think this advice is mistaken—not because the notion of speaking without notes is bad. On the contrary, I prefer that approach. The problem, though, is that for most amateur speakers, it's a great source of comfort and security to know the notes are there, just in case you forget. I've known speakers who put notes on the stand in front of them and then delivered their entire address without even so much as glancing down at them.

"Why did you take those notes up there in the first place?" I asked one woman who had obviously not had to use them.

"Because it's nice to know they're there—just in case," she replied.

I think that's as good a reason as any. But some people not only carry their notes up with them; they also refer to them regularly during the talk. What's the best way to do this, and still maintain a natural, conversational style?

Here are a few tips that have helped me and other speakers in the smooth use of notes before an audience:

Test your notes.

Try three or four dry runs by yourself or in the presence of a close friend or loved one before you ever stand up before a live audience. This is in some respects just another way of saying, once again, that you've got to practice a speech if you hope to do a good job of delivering it before a group. But it's also important, as you run through your practice sessions, to keep an eye out for

142

defects in your notes. For example, you may find you continue to stumble over one section of your written outline, and it may be necessary to clarify it or even expand it. Or more likely, after you've gone over the speech, you'll probably discover that you don't need as many notes as you thought you did. At first, you may have outlined rather extensively the anecdotes you want to tell, but after you go over them orally a few times, you find that it's only necessary to jot down the basic theme of the illustration: You might write just the "wild horse" or the "president's daughter" or the "firehouse."

Perhaps the best user of notes I know is Ronald Reagan, who keeps extensive notes for his speeches on stacks of 4 × 5-inch cards. He has gone over his stories and other points so often that his whole presentation flows extremely smoothly. When he glances down at his cards on occasion, you're hardly aware of it because he maintains a conversational flow to his speech that often gives you the impression he is carrying on a casual, one-on-one meeting with you. But there is also a danger in Reagan's approach. I've heard some people say that they feel his speeches sometimes sound "canned" or too fluent to be real. The main reason for this flaw is probably the fact that he's told his favorite anecdotes and pet phrases too often. But you really don't have to worry about this danger. You'd have to give the same speech fifty times before it would begin to sound as though you're spouting a series of slogans.

Work on your transitions.

The weakest spot in your use of notes is your ability to move easily from one major section in your speech to the next. These transition points, or links between the key

143

areas in a talk, often sound contrived or stiff in an inexperienced speaker's mouth, primarily because most beginners don't realize they have to spend a great deal of time polishing their transitions during practice sessions. In many cases, the speaker will get so involved in discussing one point with his audience that he'll find himself getting away from his notes and becoming involved in effective interaction and eye contact with his audience. But when he finishes that point, he'll falter as he tries to find his place in his notes and move on to the next big point. Unless you've worked hard on your transitions and can anticipate, after considerable practice, exactly what you're going to say and where you're going to say it, you'll find yourself stumbling over your words, searching uncomfortably through your notes, and breaking the fine pace and momentum you've established.

Write your notes legibly.

This principle may seem too obvious to mention, but I'm constantly amazed at the messy way many speakers put their notes together. And if you've written your thoughts down in a tiny, hurried scrawl, you may well find yourself saying—or feeling like saying—to your audience, "I'm sorry, but I'm afraid I can't read my own handwriting."

I think it's always best to type your notes or at least print them clearly, in easy-to-see block letters. Otherwise, you may well find yourself squinting and worrying over the very papers that should be enhancing your confidence and improving your presentation.

A variation on the notes debate is whether or not it's a good idea to write out your entire speech and deliver it from a complete script. It's with great reluctance that I get into this area because I begin with a fundamental prejudice against reading a speech. I think you can quickly become entirely conversational and natural in your delivery of a speech from a skeletal outline or a few notes. But this natural style becomes much more difficult, if not impossible, when you're tied down to speaking every word just as it is written in front of you. So even though I favor the use of notes by beginning speakers, I'm much more negative about complete scripts. In fact, my advice would be: Do everything you can to avoid giving a talk by reading a text! If you get caught in this trap, you may well bore your audience to tears—and may even succeed in putting yourself to sleep!

Having said all that, I now have to pass on a few thoughts about how to read a speech if you find you have no other choice. Sometimes, the topic you have to deal with may be so sensitive that you or others connected with your speaking assignment may feel it's advisable to have each of your statements written out precisely so that there's no chance of your making an indiscreet remark. At other times, especially if you're talking as an official spokesman of some sort, you may have to get your observations approved ahead of time, and that's possible only with a complete written text.

One of the few recent occasions when I wrote out a complete speech involved an appearance before the United Nations. And I didn't volunteer to script my talk—I was asked to submit my remarks to the State Department beforehand so that the diplomatic experts there could be sure I didn't inadvertently put my foot in my mouth.

My topic was drug abuse, and our government officials were concerned, first, that some colloquial, drug-related slang that I often use wouldn't translate properly. In other words, you can't say "freak out" in Egyptian or "off the wall" in Afghan and have those phrases come out meaning much to the foreigners. Also, American officials were afraid that if the speech weren't constructed carefully, some of the Communist nations would seize on my remarks and quote them out of context, to the detriment of the Western nations. So I wrote out the speech, and these officials examined it very closely and did some rewriting so that everything I said would be clear and yet not be vulnerable to misquoting. I was fascinated at the way they changed certain phrases and sentences and linked them to other parts of the speech so that it would be very difficult to quote me out of context and still have the quotations make sense.

But it's hard for anyone, and especially a relatively inexperienced speaker, to read a written text and still make it sound natural and conversational. As a matter of fact, some of our top radio and TV announcers are paid very good money because they have developed the ability, over a period of years, to read a script naturally. And I certainly don't expect you to acquire this skill overnight, or perhaps even in a lifetime. But I do think it's possible for you to improve your speech reading if you find yourself in a situation where this technique is required.

I've done a great deal of script reading for radio and television commercials, and I've found that the most important thing to ask yourself, right at the outset, is, "How can I fit this script into my own personal speaking style so that the words sound natural and informal?"

On a number of occasions, I've been asked by advertising agencies to read a "cutesy" commercial, and I'll just tell them, "I'm sorry, I can't read that!" There may be a number of reasons for my reluctance, and they all relate directly back to what I know I can and can't say in public if I'm going to appear to be relating conversationally with my

146

listeners. Sometimes, the agency may want me to make extravagant statements, or "puff" or "hype" a product, and I know I can't do that and make my speech sound sincere or appealing. So if I find what I consider ridiculous or unbelievable statements in the script, I insist that they be changed before I try to read them.

More frequently, the ad agency will want me to cram too many words in the minute or so I have to speak—like a schlock drugstore window, where they seem to have thrown everything from the warehouse onto the shelves. The agency people always seem to be hoping they can get two more sentences in, and they'll say, "Hey, can't you read it just a little faster?"

I say, "Of course I *could* read it faster, but that wouldn't be me. If you want somebody to read at two hundred words a minute, hire someone who reads fast. If you want me, as a personality, then I have to go at my own pace. You don't have the same record if you play it at 78 instead of 33."

I'd recommend you take a similar approach if you find yourself having to read a speech. Go over it several times to find a pace that fits your own natural speaking style and then stick to it. But there's a great deal more to reading a speech naturally than simply finding your pace. Listen to this advice from one expert, Russ Reed, a professional radio and TV announcer and actor whose many credits include doing commercials for Hallmark cards, Sears, and Standard Oil, and serving as narrator for the "Unshackled" radio program:

"If you're writing your own speech, keep in mind that some things are written to be read by the eye, and some are written to be read by the mouth," Reed says. "Any written text you write yourself or edit for your own speaking should be drafted to conform with the way you speak. When I read a script, I can tell in the first two to three sentences whether the writer is a book-writer or a script-writer skilled in dialogue. One way the amateur can write a speech for oral reading is to say it aloud as he writes it. If it doesn't sound the way you actually talk, keep rewording the text until you feel comfortable saying it out loud."

In Reed's many years of reading scripts he's come up with several guidelines for effective, conversational speech reading. You might find it helpful to use them as a checklist if you find yourself in the position of having to speak from a prepared text:

Mark the speech to conform with your speaking style.

"I use my own system of hieroglyphics to mark up a speech before I deliver it," Reed says. For example, he underlines points he wants to emphasize with a louder tone of voice, and he inserts vertical lines in the text to indicate where he wants to pause. If he wants to be sure he *won't* pause at the end of a line, he might draw a little arrow around, pointing to the following line, to indicate he should keep the flow of the speech going. If he comes across a phrase that doesn't quite fit into the narrative flow, he sets it off with parentheses. Then when he's actually speaking that phrase, he'll either toss it off by changing the tone of his voice or set it apart with some strategic pauses.

"I go over the entire speech and make these markings before I start practicing it out loud," Reed explains. "I mainly use my eyes and brain at this point to see what *should* be the most logical way to say the speech. Then after I've marked it up, I'll go over it out loud and see how it 'feels' during an oral delivery. If it seems to say what it should be saying, then it's okay and all that's left for me to do is polish it through practice."

Trust the speech after you've marked it.

Under no circumstances, Reed says, should you try to change the marked, prepared speech after you stand up to deliver it. You've already thought it through and practiced it, and if you try to do some ad hoc alterations when you're standing in front of your audience, you're bound to get into trouble. You'll use the wrong inflections, stumble over words, or make other gaffes—and there's no reason for such mistakes! Trust your preparation, and your preparation will carry you through to a successful presentation.

Learn how to read a list.

If you read a list or series of items the wrong way, you may confuse your listeners and throw off the pacing you're trying to set for yourself. In general, Reed suggests you use an upward inflection for all but the last item in a list and then make your voice go down on the last item. If your inflection is up on the last item, you won't signal adequately to your audience that you've reached the end of the list, and you'll leave them dangling, waiting for another item, which never comes. In other words, if you say, "It's important for every Boy Scout to be brave, kind, and reverent," your voice should rise upward on "brave" and "kind" but then go lower on "reverent."

Adjust your microphone for reading.

Many of the principles we've already discussed for the proper use of a microphone apply when you're reading your speech, but there are a few special points you should be aware of. Reed suggests adjusting the microphone height with an eye to the direction your mouth will be pointing as you read—or slightly lower than it might be if you were always looking up toward your audience. "You should aim it right for your mouth, and be aware that the stage manager has probably adjusted it for a six-foot guy, even though you may only be five-six."

Reed stresses that the basic principles of microphone use we've already described, such as speaking *across* the mike at all times, apply when you're reading a speech. But while you're reading there may also be a tendency to lean forward toward your notes, and this can bring you too close to the microphone for the proper audio effect. "One of the things that bugs me about speakers is that they start 'popping,' " he notes. "Their *p's* and *b's* and *ph's* start to 'pop' because they've moved too close to the mike. If you start to pop, that's a signal that you should move farther back."

Finger the script.

When Reed is reading from a script, he always keeps his finger on the text. This practice frees him to look up regularly at his audience and maintain some eye contact, then go back to the text and pick up where he left off when he looked up.

"My finger doesn't lie," Reed says. "When I look up, I always make sure that my finger is resting on the spot where I want to continue reading when I look back down. As a professional, I've learned to read about a line and a half to two lines ahead of where I'm actually speaking. So when I'm ready to look up at my audience, I'll place my finger at that point where I've read ahead to in the text." Then, when his speaking catches up with his reading, he looks back down and picks up at the word on which his finger is resting. Although Reed reads far ahead of where he's speaking, he says that even the rankest amateur should be able to learn fairly quickly to read at least four to five words ahead of his speaking, and this "lead time" should provide plenty of opportunities to look up at your audience, encourage some eye-to-eye interaction, and then go back to the script.

Use a clear, simple format for your script.

Reed suggests that you type your speech in a double-spaced format, with all the words in upper case for easy reading. As with the format for any notes you might use in a normal speech, you don't want to fall into the trap of not being able to read or understand your own writing.

Learn the basic page-turning tricks.

There's usually a pocket or shelf just below the top of the podium, and Reed finds that space handy to slip his pages into when he's finished with them. If you use this method carefully, there's no reason why anyone on your level or below you in the audience should even see a page of your script.

Russ Reed often attempts to distract his listeners as he changes pages, by looking up or even making some gesture with his free hand. He also makes certain that he transfers his pages only while he's actually speaking, not during a pause. That way, his words cover up any rustle of paper.

He also advises all speakers with a complete text to be certain that they have removed all paper clips or staples before they stand up before the audience. Otherwise, it's necessary to turn the pages of the script over in full view of the audience. In addition, the text may get unbalanced and even fall off the podium when you reach your last page and have only one page on the bottom and all the others, still attached, off to one side.

If there's no shelf under the podium, Reed suggests just shifting each page to one side as unobtrusively as possible after you're finished with it.

Go to your audience empty-handed.

If you're reading a fairly long speech, you could intimidate your listeners and maybe even drive some out of the auditorium if they see you lugging what looks like a book manuscript up to the podium. Reed prefers to have the text already on the podium before the audience arrives so that they won't be scared away and also so that they won't try to anticipate how long he's going to talk.

One cautionary note to this practice has been suggested to me by the Reverend Philip A. C. Clarke, pastor of the Park Avenue United Methodist Church in New York City. Rev. Clarke often writes out his sermons and delivers them using many of the techniques Russ Reed advocates. But he had one disastrous experience when he left his sermon text in the pulpit an hour or so ahead of time and found, to his chagrin, that someone had removed the papers, apparently in a misdirected attempt at housecleaning. He still leaves his text up in the pulpit, but now he always protects himself by carrying an extra copy of the sermon in an inside pocket.

152

Reading a speech in a natural, believable way is tough, but an even more difficult thing to do well in public speaking is to move out of a prepared text, into some ad-lib comments, then back into the written text. The person I knew who could do this kind of speaking with a sort of seamless quality so that you couldn't tell when he was reading the script and when he wasn't, was President Franklin D. Roosevelt.

I introduced FDR on the air several times, and I was astounded by the way he could read a paragraph, shift to speak off-the-cuff about some related topic, then pick right up again where he had left off reading—without a hitch or hesitation in his presentation. The only reason I knew he was moving back and forth like that was that I was following the script as he spoke. I'm sure none of his radio listeners had any idea what he was doing. They just heard a very articulate, smooth, conversational talker discussing important national issues with them as though he were sitting right next to them in an easy chair.

The most difficult aspect of shifting gears from reading to extemporaneous speaking and back to reading is your use of transitions. Unless you work hard in preparing and practicing those phrases and sentences that get you out of the written text and also back into it smoothly, your attempts to ad-lib are going to stick out like sore thumbs. There is a certain boring cadence to many written speeches, whereas speeches made from notes usually include redundancies, hesitations, and stumblings that give them a more natural sound. The only way to achieve what FDR was able to do is, first, to read your speech with some of the same halting qualities and intonations that you use when you talk off-the-cuff. Then, you also have to practice your ad-libs over and over so that they come close to the fluency of cadence that is always bound to lurk in your reading.

153

This combination of reading and ad-libbing is so hard that I would strongly advise you to avoid it until you get considerably more experience before groups. Even then, employ the technique only when, for some reason, you absolutely have to.

Having warned you about delivering various kinds of written speeches, I suppose I should also mention a related technique that's another of my pet peeves. I'm talking about the practice of memorizing a speech. Perhaps you'll find you must read a speech on occasion. But I don't believe there's *ever* any excuse for a beginner to memorize one! You may want to memorize an outline or certain major points so that you can speak without notes. But you should never, never try to memorize an entire speech, word for word!

Why am I so adamant on this point? In the first place, if you try to memorize a speech and forget one line, you're dead. You'll get flustered, flounder around, and may even find yourself standing before your audience unable to say a word. Second, memorizing a complete talk imprisons you in a very small verbal cell. You lack the flexibility to flow with your audience and to change part of your talk in midstream if you find you're losing them. Finally, almost all the memorized speeches I've heard have an artificial quality about them, even if the speaker recites each line perfectly. There's a tendency for the speaker to concentrate primarily on what he's going to say next so that he can be sure not to forget one word, rather than on the reactions of his listeners.

I would strongly advise you to use brief notes or an outline in most of your talks. At the same time, try an occasional short speech without any notes at all, just to give yourself practice with this technique. But limit speeches that you read from a text to situations where you're in effect *required* to use that method. And never, under any

154

circumstances, try to memorize an entire speech, word for word.

If you follow these guidelines, your talks will come across as much more natural, your relationship with your audiences will be much warmer, and you'll discover you have the freedom to take the "pulse" and "temperature" of your listeners and alter your presentation as the mood dictates. Good public speaking, after all, is nothing more than good private speaking projected to a larger group of listeners. So be sure that whatever notes you use enhance the personal bond of communication that's at the root of any good conversational relationship.

CHAPTER ELEVEN

⚜ ⚜ ⚜

"And Now, a Few Off-the-Cuff Remarks from . . . "

At some time in your life, you've probably faced a situation like this:

Reserved, unobtrusive Jane Jones was sitting quietly in her seat in an audience, listening to a program at her service organization, when suddenly the master of ceremonies got up and said, "You know, before we finish today, I'd like to hear about Jane Jones' recent trip to Israel, wouldn't you? Jane, could you come up and say a few words to us?"

What happens as all eyes focus expectantly on you? Probably your stomach rises into your throat the second you hear your name; your hands grow cold; beads of perspiration appear on your forehead or upper lip; and you may even feel faint. You've been caught unprepared, and most likely you'll start out with, "I really don't know what to say." And you may well end up spouting out a confused, nervous garble of non sequiturs.

But this needn't be the case. With just a little information and preparation, which you can learn about as you're reading this chapter, you can be well on your way to developing into an adequate extemporaneous speaker. I'm *not* saying I can turn you into an off-the-cuff orator who can give a well-organized, moving half-hour address on a moment's notice. Only highly experienced speakers can do that. But you *can* learn rather quickly to speak for a few minutes in a coherent, informative, and even funny or inspirational way if you'll just take a few moments with me to learn how to go about it.

The basic principle in speaking off-the-cuff is that you always try to avoid doing it off-the-cuff. I don't mean you should refuse to speak when asked to—just that you should try to *anticipate* situations where you may be asked to speak and then prepare ahead of time to give a short talk in case you are called upon.

I call this approach "prepared extemporaneous speaking"—a phrase that may seem a contradiction in terms, but which I believe is actually the best way to speak effectively off-the-cuff. And I'm not suggesting that this method should be limited to amateur speakers either. Most of the top professional platform speakers I know prepare in advance if they're going to be attending a party, banquet, or other function where they think there's even the slightest chance that they might be called upon to say a few words.

For example, as I mentioned in my book *Yes, You Can!* I was invited to attend a dinner at the White House honoring Prince Charles of Great Britain, and I found myself sitting next to Bob Hope and the American Ambassador to Great

Britain, Jock Whitney. I hadn't been asked to speak, but I knew there was a chance I might be called on since President Nixon was an old friend and had invited me there. So I spent some time preparing a few remarks and selecting some appropriate stories.

As it turned out, I wasn't asked to say anything and neither was Hope or Whitney. On an impulse, I asked them afterward, "I'm curious—did you prepare anything to say tonight, just in case you might be asked to speak?"

Hope laughingly admitted, "Are you kidding, Art— I'm always ready!" And Whitney, who is not a professional speaker, said he had been unable to get to sleep the previous night until he had settled on some appropriate remarks to make in the event he was called up to the podium.

Now any of the three of us, with no prior preparation at all, could probably have done a creditable job if we had been tapped at that dinner. I speak so often that I actually carry in my head about six hours worth of fairly polished speeches and jokes on a variety of subjects. Yet each of us, with all our experience, felt compelled to spend a little extra time selecting and fine-tuning a few words for that dinner—an event where none of us had been given any inkling that we might have to speak.

The lesson for you from this example is that if you're relatively inexperienced as a speaker, you should devote at least a little time to contingency planning for possible extemporaneous speaking situations. The more you can anticipate those times when you may be called on for some public remarks, the less you'll have to worry about being caught off guard and embarrassed. Also, the better impression you'll make as a well-spoken, articulate person.

In learning to speak extemporaneously, I find it's helpful to think in terms of two situations: (1) those that you anticipate and prepare for beforehand; and (2) those that you've failed to prepare for and where you find yourself having to "wing it" by speaking completely off the top of your head. Two different speaking techniques are necessary for these two different situations, so let's examine each in turn to see exactly what will be required of you.

1. How to Anticipate an Extemporaneous Speech.

If you're really serious about becoming a good off-the-cuff speaker, I would advise you to take a moment or two at the beginning of each day (or perhaps during the prior evening) to go over your daily schedule and see what kinds of gatherings you may be attending where you could be asked to say a few words. It's at this point that most people fail at "prepared extemporaneous speaking" because if you haven't been formally invited to speak or warned in advance that you'll probably be called on, the tendency is to think, "It's too much trouble to try to prepare something. I probably won't be asked to say anything, so I'll just take a chance and not worry about it."

You can call this attitude procrastination, a lack of self-discipline, or whatever at this point. But your feelings will quickly turn into embarrassment and a mental kicking of yourself if you *are* called on and fail to perform up to par. So why not make speech anticipation a regular part of your daily routine?

It takes only a few moments to identify those two or three business meetings or social gatherings each day where you may be asked to make a few remarks. And then it will require only an extra minute or two to jot down a key point or anecdote you might want to use in case you're called upon. I would estimate that with *no more than five minutes of such preparation each day,* you could improve your off-the-cuff speaking performance by five hundred percent!

Let me give you an example from the experience of a man—call him "Charlie Smith"—who took my advice on this technique. Charlie, a New Yorker, had been invited to stay with some friends in Texas in a town where he had attended high school. After he arrived at their house, he learned they would all be attending a special service that evening at a church he had attended as a boy. Suddenly, something clicked in his mind that made him think, "I might be called on to say something at that meeting."

So he spent a minute or two while he was in the shower going over possible remarks he might make. He finally decided that if he was called on, he would open with a reference to the church and then use a short joke I had told him:

"I was feeling pretty positive—and even rather young—until I walked through the front door and heard somebody say, 'You know, that looks a lot like the *late* Charlie Smith.' "

Not the greatest joke in the world, but it was certainly adequate to use if he was called on for some off-the-cuff remarks. And sure enough, he *was* called on, and he did a decent job with his joke and a few other positive observations he made about the progress of the church. Total preparation time? Maybe three minutes of thought without writing down one word. Yet his performance was far superior to what it would have been if he hadn't taken those three minutes to do a little anticipation.

Another area where it's easy to anticipate is where you think you might be called on—or want to volunteer—to give a toast. There are plenty of speaking books that contain lists of appropriate toasts for a variety of different occasions, and you might want to purchase one of these for reference before you attend a dinner or party. Or if you take a minute or so to anticipate, you'll probably be able to come up with an original, personalized toast that's more appropriate for the occasion than anything you can find in a book. By preparing a toast beforehand, you not only make yourself look good in public, you also make the individual who is the object of the toast *feel* good because you've come up with just the right words for him or her on this special occasion.

But no matter how much you try to anticipate possible speaking situations, you can't always be prepared for every contingency. Sometimes, you're bound to get caught off guard—but that doesn't mean you have to fall on your face. Let's take a look now at some techniques that can help you respond well to a totally unexpected request to speak publicly.

2. How to Speak Entirely Off-the-Cuff.

If you've failed to identify a possible public speaking situation in advance, or if you just didn't take time one day even to try to anticipate, all is not lost! The challenge facing you is more difficult, but you can still do a decent job on your feet if you just keep calm and go through a simple mental procedure for on-the-spot speech preparation.

Some of the principles for this kind of totally extemporaneous speaking are the same as those used for the extemporaneous speaking games in the "Forensic Family" chapter. You may want to refer back to that section at this time.

Here's the brief mental procedure I go through when I'm caught off guard:

- Begin at the end. As you're walking up to the platform, fix your mind on the topic you've been asked to speak about. Settle immediately on the conclusion you want to reach. Don't worry at this point about how you're going to get there.
- Next, select one or two, or at the most three, points you want to make that relate directly to your conclusion. Think of a simple word or phrase that describes those points, and don't clutter up your mind with any of the details that may qualify or describe each point.
- Select a brief, simple, straightforward opening that describes what you hope to say. It's also helpful to attach some pleasant reference to your audience, such as how happy and honored you are to be with them. Don't get tricky! If you try to tell a story or a joke, you'll probably stumble all over yourself. You've been caught off guard, and your main line of defense must be to simplify, simplify, simplify!
- If you have a minute or so before you actually have to speak, run over in your mind your conclusion, those one to three main points, and finally your opening.
- In the very last second or so, before you actually open your mouth, concentrate solely on your opening remarks—and nothing else. The chances are, if you get started smoothly, you'll move fairly easily through the short talk you've constructed in your head.

Suppose, for example, you are at a dinner of good friends who are celebrating a couple's wedding anniversary. Suddenly the host pops up and calls on you, as a long-time friend of the guests of honor, for a toast or a few comments on the significance of this date.

What you should first do is to settle on your conclusion—perhaps that this couple is the happiest example of wedded bliss among all the people you know, but that they had to learn many tough lessons from life to reach this state. Then, quickly decide on the one to three main points that will lead to this conclusion; and finally, think of a simple opening that introduces these points.

For example, with a twinkle-of-the-eye and a tongue-in-cheek attitude, you might begin by relating an actual (or imaginary) story that involved a date during the couple's courtship in a leaky, rented rowboat in a public park on a spring day. From there, you might go on to describe an embarrassing predicament, such as the boy losing both oars, falling overboard, getting the boat caught in a sandbar, and ruining the girl's new spring dress. Then, you could go on to pay a tribute to how she began at this point to learn great understanding and patience toward her husband-to-be. And with tongue still in cheek, you might mention how they both immediately realized they were a very compatible pair, with her goodnaturedness acting to offset his clumsiness. Finally, you could conclude by saying that a series of such husband-inspired mishaps and angelic wifely responses over the years have resulted in the happy couple you see before you—"Indeed, here was a match made in heaven!"

If you can come up with a brief mental outline like this on a familiar topic in a few seconds, you'll be in extremely good shape to deliver a decent impromptu talk. And you *can* do it! All it takes is a decision on your part to follow the simple procedure I've outlined immediately after you're asked to speak. Don't waste time playing coy or refusing to speak. Assume from the outset that you're going to respond positively to the invitation and then get those wheels turning in your brain!

Of course, if you can buy a little time by asking your host for a "formal" introduction or otherwise delay your actual speaking for a moment or so to give you time to put your thoughts in order, so much the better. But whatever you do, don't let any opportunity to speak under these circumstances pass you by. If you take up the challenge and try to speak in these tough conditions a few times, you'll find yourself getting better and better—and you'll probably even start looking forward to being put on the spot before a group of strangers.

I believe experienced extemporaneous speakers actually begin to develop "grooves" or "connections" in their brains —tracks that they have been over several times and that become easier and easier to travel the more they speak off-the-cuff. So much of effective public speaking is being able to make smooth transitions, change your responses to the needs of your audience, and toss out little remarks and gestures that give your presentation a polished, professional look. These techniques evolve only with practice and experience. You have to speak many times to groups before those "grooves" in your brain are sufficiently deep or well developed that the words flow along smoothly and effortlessly.

The first few attempts you make at extemporaneous speaking may be good enough that they'll surprise you if you follow the procedures I've outlined in this chapter. But after about fifty such speeches, you'll get even better, as you hop up onto another plateau of expertise.

It's rather like learning to type. I won some typing contests when I was a kid and actually earned a living briefly as a secretary. At first, I was able to type reasonably well, but I had to *think* about where the various letters and numbers were and which fingers would strike the right keys. After a little more practice, though, I found I could see the sentence, "The quick brown fox jumped over the fence," and before I knew it, those words would be on the typing paper before me. I didn't have the slightest idea how they got there, though. I did know my typing skills had something to do with practice and with conditioning my eyes to control my fingers through some part of my brain that was outside my consciousness. And even more important, I understood that to maintain or improve upon those skills, I had to continue to do plenty of typing.

Similar principles apply to extemporaneous public speaking. As I'm talking now in off-the-cuff situations, I don't really think of each word or phrase as I say it. I'm always looking ahead, asking myself, "Shall I take that road or this—tell that story or cite this statistic?" It's almost like walking down a path you already know. Your eyes search the landscape forty feet ahead of you because you know, without even looking, what to expect of the ground on which you're treading. You may occasionally glance down at your feet, but generally the feet take care of the familiar bumps and depressions by themselves. In the same way, when I'm before a group, I'm always mentally looking just ahead as I speak. I may be going over a completely familiar path or, in an impromptu situation, I may have to strike out on a somewhat different route, but there's always some well-known signpost or landmark that enables me to keep moving purposefully and logically toward my conclusion.

You can't expect to have complete command of all the necessary transitions and turns of phrase when you start doing extemporaneous speaking. But as you add to your experience, you'll find you get more competent—and confident—in responding to that inherently nerve-racking call, "And now, a few off-the-cuff remarks from . . . "

CHAPTER TWELVE

How to Survive an Introduction

The best introduction for a speech is a short introduction, and in keeping with that fine tradition, I'm going to keep this chapter very short. Actually, there are only a couple of things that need to be said about introducing a speaker, and even though it doesn't take very long to say them, these points are extremely important. You should keep these principles right at the front of your mind, both if you are asked to give an introduction and also if you have a chance to brief the person who has been assigned to introduce you.

First, you should avoid a long, flowery, complimentary introduction. Above all, never promise too much:

"Here, ladies and gentlemen, is one of the most interesting people in the whole world. She's going to give you one of the funniest talks you've heard in your whole life!" Anyone who has to follow this kind of introduction is in deep trouble. The audience has in effect been encouraged to think, "Oh yeah? Well, let's just see how good this speaker really is!"

If you're unfortunate enough to be introduced this way, I would suggest you try to come up with some preliminary remarks to reestablish your modesty and reduce your image to something less than superhuman dimensions. You might say something like, "Wow, after hearing that introduction, I almost checked to see if I didn't show up on the wrong night!"

Even if you really *are* a famous, outstanding, almost superhuman personality, it's still best to speak after a low-key introduction. Eleanor Roosevelt understood this principle, and she always asked those introducing her to keep their preliminary remarks as short and simple as possible. Usually, this request worked quite well. But one old crusty farmer who was chosen to introduce her in one county meeting took her too literally. He got up and said, "Ladies and gentlemen, here's Eleanor Roosevelt—the less said about her, the better!"

The second key element in a good introduction is that it shouldn't detract from the main event, which is the speaker who is being introduced. One very damaging thing that the introducer can do is "pull the strings" on one of the speaker's best remarks. For example, I might be planning on opening with a reference to the fact that I was an orphan, abandoned in the little town of Moose Jaw and adopted by a preacher. This lead gets me into some of my preacher jokes. But if the guy who is introducing me says, "Our speaker tonight was an orphan who was adopted by a preacher when he was an infant," the lead-in to my opening jokes is gone.

Rather than put yourself in the position of having to revise your opening at the last minute to compensate for this kind of introduction, it's best to pull the introducer aside and say, "I'm wondering if you could give me some idea of just what you're going to say, because there are a couple of things I'd like to have you mention which could really help my talk, but which won't rob it of any points I plan to make."

The person assigned to introduce you is usually more than happy to get some direction about what he should say. But just be sure you don't fluster the person by hitting him in the last few seconds with some ideas about his introduction that invalidate everything he's prepared. That could in effect put him in the position of having to make a short extemporaneous speech himself to accommodate you. To assist your introducer, you might type out a few remarks for him before you even arrive in the auditorium so that he won't have to rush about putting together a new set of notes for himself.

Of course, sometimes there's not a thing you can do about influencing the introducer to do the kind of job that's going to enhance the impact of your speech. In that case, you just have to try to repair the damage with a few preliminary remarks yourself. Or, in the most extreme case, you might even be tempted to do what Will Rogers once did.

It seems he was asked to deliver a speech to a social club, and the chairman of the club, who saw the occasion as his own chance to shine, prepared an introduction almost as long as Will's talk. When he finally finished, he said, "And now here is Mr. Will Rogers with his address for the night."

Will stood up and said, "My address is 1012 East Fifth Street, St. Louis, Missouri. Good night!"

I seriously doubt that you'll face this sort of extreme situation, and I'm not sure I'd ever suggest that you refuse to give a talk simply because of a poor introduction. But this story always serves to remind me that introductions, whether I'm giving them or on the receiving end, are more important than most people realize. So if you're asked to introduce someone, always remember that you're not the star, you're presenting the star. Prepare a few succinct, punchy remarks with this principle in mind. And if you have the misfortune to follow a bad introduction, do your best to repair the damage (without being vindictive or nasty) in your opening and then *forget* the introduction. Forge ahead with such a forceful speech that your listeners won't even remember how you got up to the podium!

⚓ ⚓ ⚓

Some
Inside Information
on Inspiration

W hen you first start out as a public speaker, I would suggest you keep everything as simple and straightforward as possible. Avoid jokes. Avoid tricky gestures or props. Avoid anything that might confuse you or require you to strain your speaking powers beyond your present capacity.

And this list of things to avoid includes so-called inspirational speaking as well. By "inspirational" I mean doing or saying things that will cause an audience to cry, catch its breath, or soar along with you on wings of enthusiasm. Those first few talks you give should focus on information, not inspiration. They should focus on unadorned communication and gentle persuasion, not the evocation of deep emotion.

But as I said in discussing jokes, I know you're eventually going to want to try your hand at a little inspiration. So rather than let you fly off on your own on some cloud of soppy, corny sentimentality, I want to provide you with a primer on effective inspirational speaking. But use it sparingly! Too heavy an emphasis on evoking deep emotions—especially if you're inexperienced—carries some of the same dangers as hitting your audience with too many jokes. They may quickly become bored with your efforts, and you'll be in a worse position than if you had just kept away altogether from attempts at inspiration or humor.

Inspiration in public speaking almost always depends on storytelling. One exception might include inspiration in a political speech, where, like William Jennings Bryan a few chapters back, you crystallize the thoughts and emotions of your listeners in just the right words and lead them from cheer to cheer with appropriate crescendos and inflections in your tone of voice. Another exception is the exhoratory speech, which you might deliver as a sermon in your church to get your listeners to change their way of living or at your Kiwanis or Rotary Club when you ask them to follow you in some worthwhile service project. In this case, it would take just the right balance in emphasis—not too accusatory to alienate them, yet sufficiently authoritative that they'll be ready to stop what they're doing and follow you.

But these are specialized kinds of inspiration. What we're concerned with in this chapter is a *classic* form of inspiration that you might insert briefly into a regular speech to make a point. And as I said, the best way of doing

172

that is through relating an appropriate, emotion-evoking anecdote.

There are five basic elements I've identified for most effective inspirational stories, and I now want to spend a few moments sharing them with you:

Element 1:
Keep to the basic time limits for any story or anecdote.

We saw in Chapter Four that most good oral stories (*not* jokes) run at least a minute in the telling, and usually no longer than two minutes.

Element 2:
Maintain a relatively slow pace.

I might rattle off a funny story in a bright, rather quick rush of words. But to set the mood for an inspirational story—especially a sad one that has the potential of moving your audience to tears—you have to put on your verbal brakes.

Element 3:
Use a sad, pensive, or conversational tone of voice.

It's difficult to convey all the dimensions of this principle in print. Let me try to illustrate what I mean.

Suppose your subject is the importance of caring: "There was a pathetic little girl . . . behind the orphanage . . . who hid something in the cleft of a tree. A teacher, spying on the furtive act, said, 'There's that miserable child no one ever plays with. She's probably been stealing something from the other kids, and she's hiding it in that little place in the tree. I'll get her!' . . . When the little girl left, the teacher could hardly wait to get down there. But when she reached the tree, all she found was a wrinkled slip of paper . . . on which that little girl had scrawled: 'Whoever finds this . . . I love you!' "

Now, in relating this little vignette orally, I would slow my voice down, especially at those points where there are extra periods in the written text. Look back over the story and review this point. The more deliberate pace allows the words to sink in and begin to work on the emotions of my listeners. I'd assume a slightly grave, even sad tone in the last sentence, and if my eyes naturally water a little, so much the better. But don't fake it! If your own honest emotion doesn't evoke tears, use a poignant pause.

Element 4:
Have a sincere, personal belief in the inspirational value of your story.

This point may be the most important because if you're merely trying to manipulate the emotions of your listeners and you don't believe a word of what you're saying, you're going to come across as a total cornball! On the other hand, if you *really believe* in what you're saying, you'll be in a much stronger position to make an inspirational impact, even if your presentation of the anecdote is somewhat amateurish.

Sincerity is the key that unlocks inspiration as well as persuasion.

Element 5:
Use a classic inspirational "story line."

I react negatively to most cut-and-dried formulas in speech making, so I offer this final principle of inspirational storytelling with some hesitation. There are many ways to tell a good inspirational story, just as there are many ways to tell a good joke, and any rules we try to lay down automatically bring to mind a spate of exceptions.

Still, there is some validity in citing formulas if you take them as general guidelines, rather than hard-and-fast rules. So here goes:

One classic structure for a good inspirational or emotion-evoking story is the *surprise ending story*, which is similar in form to that of a good joke. You'll recall that most effective jokes catch the listener off guard, with some incongruous or offbeat ending that tickles his funny bone. The same principle applies with the inspirational story line, except that the surprise often results in sadness, or a "rush" of good feelings, rather than laughter. The short story I just related about the little orphan girl is an example of this approach, with the unexpected note in the tree being the surprise.

Another approach to inspirational storytelling, which is somewhat more complex, is based on what has been called the "inverted bell-curve" structure. This is a formula that has been used to explain the construction and emotional impact of longer inspirational stories, such as those found in *Guideposts* magazine and the *Reader's Digest*.

175

The basic idea is that the speaker or writer starts off with a person in a reasonably stable or happy position, then plunges him into a crisis (the lower part of the inverted bell curve), and finally, through a spiritual renewal or other uplifting insight, brings him up again to an even higher emotional plane than the one on which he began.

Let me illustrate this inverted bell principle by using a story out of my own syndicated radio series, "The Art of Positive Thinking":

Kenny Daniels was a happy, handsome youngster who played soccer and basketball at Rosary High School in Kirkwood, Missouri, and was looking forward to a successful senior year when he lost his left leg to cancer. A tragedy, you say? The end of youthful dreams? Well, yes and no!

Of course it was a tragedy, but it was not the end of his youthful dreams. Kenny decided to face his difficult situation head on. He went to a doctor who specialized in prosthetic devices and was fitted with an artificial limb and began kicking a football.

It was painful. He was erratic, and the ball didn't go very far at first; but after months of place kicking, Kenny was ready to try out for the football team at Rosary High School. On the night of the first game Kenny was proud to be wearing the school colors. He confidently kicked field goals before the game as cheerleaders cheered and spectators filled the stadium. Most of them were unaware of the long personal struggle of the boy on the field.

No, he didn't get to kick a field goal in that first game, nor the second or third, but finally in the fifth game Kenny entered the game with eight seconds to play and the score was tied thirteen all. The ball was snapped and placed on the tee. The kicker moved forward with a slight limp, noticeable only if you knew. The ball split the uprights!

Young people like Kenny Daniels do not have "give up" in their vocabulary. They are the embodiment of this quote from Sophocles: "Heaven never helps the man who will not act!"

When you're preparing a written anecdote for presentation as part of a real speech, you have to work on the pacing, dialogue, and tone of your delivery for maximum inspirational impact. And the oral delivery would, of course, have to be much shorter than the written version to keep it within the required two-minute time limit.

Before you try telling an inspirational story, I would strongly suggest that you spend some time monitoring your own emotions. For example, pay close attention to your feelings when you go to a movie or play, watch a dramatic presentation on television, or listen to good speeches that contain moving anecdotes. If you feel yourself getting "choked up," stop for a moment and ask yourself, "Why did I react that way?" Try to identify as precisely as possible the exact words, phrases, inflections, or situations that brought tears to your eyes or a lump to your throat. The more you become aware of how inspirational material affects you personally, the better prepared you'll be to employ the same techniques to affect the emotions of others.

One friend of mine who has tried this self-monitoring method said that he got choked up several times while watching the Broadway musical *Annie*. On every occasion, the cause of his emotional reaction was related to points where Orphan Annie, the little waif who started out with everything against her, was able to triumph over all obstacles and evils. At several points in the play, she convinced industrial magnate Oliver Warbucks and even

177

top politicians like President Franklin D. Roosevelt to follow her simple belief that right and justice should win out.

In monitoring his emotions at these critical points in the play, my friend learned, among other things, the basic principle that the victory of an innocent child over seemingly insuperable odds can be a powerful element in inspiration. There are many other factors that may also go into a good inspirational story, and you'll find that the more you examine your own reactions, the more you'll learn about what works and what doesn't.

I should add one qualification here, however: If you're the kind of person who never cries and, in fact, is never moved by sad or inspirational stories, you would do well to find someone who is more emotional (perhaps your spouse) and question him or her about those tears you see trickling down the face. But perhaps an even better piece of advice to the unemotional reader would be this: Stay away from inspirational stories altogether! If you're incapable of feeling anything yourself, you're probably going to be wide of the mark in trying to tap the wellsprings of emotion in others.

Remember: You should always speak from your strengths, not your weaknesses. And if you find you're personally just not interested or moved by jokes or inspirational anecdotes or any other special form of storytelling or style of speaking, don't force yourself. Stick with what you're most interested in and what you naturally do best.

❦ ❦ ❦

Questions
and Answers

M ost of the speeches you'll be asked to give will probably require that you focus on presenting a straight talk on a subject without any direct interaction or dialogue with your audience. But there's always a chance that your host will collar you as you're about to sit down and say, "That was such an interesting talk. Do you suppose you'd have time to answer a few questions from the floor?"

And of course you'll have to agree unless you have some pressing engagement elsewhere. So how should you approach this give-and-take phase of your speech? And if you've been sitting patiently in the audience waiting for the opportunity to inject a question or objection, how should you go about it?

Even though the question-and-answer part of public speaking is often tacked onto the end of the main talk as a rather unimportant appendage, I've found that this part of my presentations can turn into the most important communication I have with my audiences. In fact, in smaller groups of, say, one hundred to three hundred people, I really love the question-and-answer periods because they give me a chance to strike out through little short bursts in new, unexpected directions. And also, the questions reflect the unspoken needs and wants of an audience that I may not have anticipated in my regular preparation. I've found on a number of occasions that I can assume my listeners want to know all about one particular subject, and I'll prepare my talk that way. But when we reach the question-and-answer session, the responses from the audience open up an area in which I may have had no idea they were interested.

I'll never forget one time when I addressed a group of women on the general subject "A Morning with Art Linkletter." With a broad topic like that, I could head in any direction I wanted, but I tried to narrow the subject down a little by asking the chairperson of the organization, "What do you think these women would like to hear about?"

She replied, "I noticed you sometimes talk about the famous women you've interviewed in your lifetime—Greer Garson, Irene Dunn, Sally Rand, Eleanor Roosevelt . . . people like that. That's marvelous stuff, and I think our people would be quite interested in it."

So that's exactly what I talked about, and when we opened up the floor for questions, I said, "I'd be happy to hear any questions you'd like to ask about people I've overlooked—Lana Turner, Marilyn Monroe, Rita Hayworth, or any other celebrities I know."

But the first woman who put up her hand had other things in mind. She asked, "I have a sixteen-year-old boy, and I think he's smoking pot. What should I tell him?"

Although I was somewhat taken off guard, I quickly recovered and started delving into my experience with kids and drugs. Then another woman put her hand up and said, "I have a boy who wants to quit high school and get a job. He doesn't care anything about school. What do you think I should tell him?"

The next woman asked, "I suspect my little boy is setting fires in our neighborhood, and I'm wondering how you think I should approach him about this?"

The questions kept coming in rapid-fire order, but not a single one had anything to do with famous people in Hollywood. These women were concerned about their families, their homes and their personal problems, and because they knew I spoke on these subjects, they decided to see if they could get any help.

Fortunately, we had arranged to have a question-and-answer period almost as long as my speech, so I was able to speak directly to those concerns that were closest to the hearts of my listeners that day. The chairman had obviously given me a completely wrong steer about the interests of the audience, but the question-and-answer session saved the day. Without that direct personal interaction, I would never have been able to take an accurate "pulse" of the vital interests of that group. So I regard the questions at the end of my talks as an extremely valuable part of the entire presentation.

But of course, when you throw open the floor to questions, you relinquish a certain amount of control over your speech. You're no longer the only one whose voice is

181

being heard in the auditorium. Anybody else who wants to raise his hand also has the right to ask or say anything that pleases him. So what should you do if you find yourself confronting a person who has just asked a bad or obnoxious question, or has decided that he wants to deliver a mini-speech in rebuttal to some of your points?

The central principle I always try to keep in mind—and sometimes it's hard when the question put to you is particularly hostile—is that you should never embarrass anybody in the audience. It's all right to be firm with a person, especially if he's in effect threatening to take over the podium from you, but don't humiliate him.

Along this line, I would highly recommend against your using any devices tht nightclub comics sometimes use to quell drunks. The classic one that Joe E. Lewis used to use against an obstreperous woman in his audience was to say, "Hey, lady, why are you trying to wreck my act when I haven't done anything to you? I don't go over to your house at night and turn off the red light on the porch."

You may get a laugh from a remark like that, and you may also succeed in forcing the person in the audience not to speak up again. But there's also a strong possibility that a substantial segment of the audience may begin to regard you as a wise guy who is using his superior position as featured speaker to put down a relatively defenseless listener.

So try to be firm but gentle when a question is off the mark or somewhat obnoxious, and you'll come out ahead in the long run. For example, in one talk I was giving on drug abuse, a person asked, "I hear that you were a good friend of Richard Nixon's. What do you think of him?"

On its face this question was totaly irrelevant because it had absolutely nothing to do with drug abuse. And the tone suggested that the person asking the question was looking for a verbal fight. But I restrained myself and replied, "The flow of our discussion is in another direction, and I don't want to divert our attention to a completely unrelated issue. But I will say I not only *was* a friend, but I *am* a friend. He's a person who admittedly has made some serious mistakes, but what friend of yours or mine hasn't?" Then I went immediately to the next question and guided the conversation back to the central topic of drug abuse.

On other occasions, when asked a similar question, I've taken another tack. Instead of meeting the questioner's challenge head-on, I'd say, "Yes, former President Nixon was a friend, and he gave me a good opportunity to fight the problem of drug abuse, which is the subject we're talking about now. He appointed me to a federal commission against drug abuse, and now let me take a few moments to descibe to you some of the things we were able to do. . . ."

In other words, I took the hostile question and turned it around to make a more positive point that was directly related to the subject of my talk. I think this technique tends to pull an audience over to your side, even though they may be in basic agreement with the negative position that the questioner is expressing. People always show respect for the speaker who takes the high road and avoids personal confrontations in a public forum. It takes some time to learn how to master this technique, but I'd highly recommend that you make this approach to fielding questions your ultimate goal.

But what if you're on the other side, asking the questions? Many people I know allow their great fear of public speaking to spill over into the question-and-answer sessions even when they're sitting in the audience. In short, they're petrified at the thought of raising their hands to ask the speaker even a short question—one that can always be framed in a sentence or two—to clear up a point that may be bothering them.

It's a shame that many people are shackled by this fear because they may fail to raise an issue that will benefit not only them but the entire audience as well. What's at the root of this fear? Sometimes, a person may worry that the question he wants to ask is stupid, but he's not sure so he decides not to take a chance on looking foolish. At other times, he may feel his question is reasonable and valid, but he feels intimidated by the speaker, who seems to have a sharp tongue and may try to get a laugh at the questioner's expense.

These fears for the most part are groundless. I've found that if you follow a relatively simple procedure in formulating a question for a speaker, you'll minimize the chance of exposing yourself to any embarrassment. And you'll also put yourself in a very strong position to look bright and intelligent in the eyes of the audience and the speaker as well. Here's the way it works:

Step 1:
Listen closely to the entire speech.

By this point in the book, you may be thinking, "This Linkletter sometimes seems determined to belabor the obvious!" And I agree that on occasion I do give advice that may *seem* obvious. But in this case, as in a number of others we've discussed, you'd be amazed at how many people ask silly, stupid questions for the simple reason that they haven't listened to everything the speaker has said. As a matter of fact, if I had to pick one major flaw in questions I get from the floor, it's this one. And I would guess that those speakers who do resort to ridiculing questioners in the audience do so, more often than not, out of frustration that the person just hasn't been listening closely.

I've had people get up, after I've devoted ten or more minutes to my views on marijuana, and ask, "Say, what do you think about marijuana?"

When this happens, I sometimes feel like throwing up my hands and saying, "What's it all for? What's the point in my even being up here?"

But instead, I usually say, "I went all through that, but I'll reiterate briefly for your benefit: I don't think marijuana is as bad as we originally thought it was, but it certainly is far, far from harmless. . . ."

But you should never put the speaker in the position of having to strain to be nice to you. Often, people don't listen closely to what the speaker has said because their minds are churning, formulating what *they* are going to say. The problem with this attitude is that there's only one speaker each night, and that's the person behind the podium. The members of the audience are there to listen, and if that's your role, be sure you're living up to it before you try any questions.

Step 2:
Write your question down on a slip of paper.

I've recommended in earlier chapters that you shouldn't write out a speech and read it from a script. But the rule for asking questions from the floor is just the opposite. Never trust your memory! If you do, and ten or fifteen minutes pass before the time for the question-and-answer session arrives, you may well find that as you open your mouth to raise an issue, the point of what you were going to say has completely escaped you. I've had dozens of people stand before me and start rambling, "I . . . you . . . weren't you saying . . . there was a part of your talk back there . . . I don't quite remember it . . . I don't agree with you. . . ."

There's no reason to get into this embarrassing situation! All you have to do is just jot down the question you want to ask when it pops into your mind during the speech—and then continue to listen closely. If the speaker covers the point later in his talk, cross it out. If he doesn't, you'll know you have a valid issue to raise, which you don't have to worry about forgetting because it's right there in front of you, in black and white.

Step 3:
Limit your question to one or two sentences.

I'm not sure there's ever any justification for using more than two sentences to raise an issue with a speaker, and more often than not, one sentence will do the job. If you disagree with what he's said, you can make that clear in a short statement and then ask him to respond to some specific point you want to make. But don't try to become a speaker yourself. You'll probably just bore the rest of the audience and make yourself look foolish in the bargain.

Step 4:
If possible, open your question with a phrase that is complimentary to the speaker.

It's important to appear pleasant and civilized even if you disagree with everything the speaker has said. Also, the contrary point you want to make will seem stronger if you're able to concede that there was at least something worthwhile in what the speaker said or the way he said it. Confronting any speaker in a hostile or strident tone may make the other members of the audience feel embarrassed for the speaker since he's an invited guest, and this approach may also set you up for a put-down you would richly deserve.

So you might start out a question with something like this: "Mr. Kissinger, your talk tonight answered a lot of questions I've had about Egypt and its potential for establishing a long-term peace with Israel. But I'm wondering if the different religions in the two countries—the Muslim faith in Egypt and Judaism in Israel—may not prove to be a big obstacle to peace?"

In this example, you've complimented Kissinger for his ability to convey important information to his audience, but you're also raising an issue he didn't cover—and you're accomplishing the entire thing in only two sentences.

Step 5:
Limit yourself to only one additional question after your main question.

Many people get so enthusiastic after they've asked one good question that they are tempted to try to launch a fullblown debate with the speaker. Resist this temptation! Remember once again: You're not the speaker and you're only one of many members of an audience. If you want to pursue a topic in greater depth, try to catch the speaker after his talk for a somewhat longer private chat. But don't monopolize the time of everybody else just to pursue one of your pet topics. If a person has posed a particularly interesting or complex question which requires a little additional expansion, I always welcome one "addendum" question. I think everyone can benefit from that. But anything more, except in the most unusual cases, tends to get tiresome.

These are the basic principles I've found most helpful in successful question-and-answer sessions, but before we leave this topic, I should mention one related speaking situation—the discussion group. You may be asked to deliver a short talk, usually to a relatively small group of a dozen or so people, and then to open your topic to an extensive discussion. This situation differs from the normal question-and-answer sessions following a regular speech because (1) you'll have to allow more time and leeway for individuals to converse with you; and (2) you'll have to elicit some of the important points you want to make from the discussion since you most likely won't have time to go into great detail during the introductory talk you give.

In some ways this kind of speaking situation is one of the most difficult because you automatically lose control over the precise direction of your presentation as additional people begin to take an active part. I've found that it's best to follow a modified version of the approach that the old Greek philosopher Socrates used—the so-called Socratic dialogue. That technique first involves doing extensive preparation yourself so that you know your subject cold. Then you ask incisive, provocative questions that draw out responses from your listeners and eventually lead to the important points you want to make.

It's extremely important to "go with the flow" in a discussion situation like this and not try to impose all your preconceptions on your listeners or force them to move with you along a rigid path toward a certain conclusion. If you don't remain flexible, you're very likely to find your audience staring at you blankly instead of responding; or they may get so frustrated that they start trying to wrest control of the discussion away from you. Watch out for a question like, "What exactly are you getting at?" Or, "What are you looking for from us?" If your listeners start responding this way, you'll know you're beginning to lose them because you're imposing your ideas on them instead of moving into your points through *their* ideas and responses.

In this situation, the tables are turned in a sense because it becomes all-important for the speaker to take plenty of time in preparing the questions he plans to ask of his audience. Like questions from the floor, they should be short and nonabrasive and you should write them down exactly as you want to ask them. And don't expect to do a perfect job in this difficult combination of speaking and discussion leading the first few times you try it. You can do an acceptable job the first time out if you prepare thoroughly. But like any other speaking, it takes practice, practice, practice to develop the facility and freedom that characterizes the really expert discussion leader.

And now the time has arrived to get even more specific. You have most of the basic tools to give a good speech in almost every situation that you're likely to confront. But there are also some highly specialized speaking situations in which even beginning speakers are likely to find themselves, and I now want to introduce you to some of the tricks of the trade in those areas.

PART III

❧ ❧ ❧

The Finer Points of Public Speaking for Private People

CHAPTER FIFTEEN

❧ ❧ ❧

*Some Lessons
from the Pulpit*

I grew up as the adopted son of a Baptist minister, so
from my earliest youth I had many opportunities to
observe at close quarters some very good and some very
bad sermons. Also, I've spent a lot of time in more recent
years in the company of some of the world's premier
preachers, like Norman Vincent Peale, Robert Schuller,
and Billy Graham. I've watched them and evaluated them
from my own perspective as a professional speaker, and
I've become convinced that these preachers have a lot to
teach a beginner about the principles of effective public
speaking.

Listen to what the great preacher Norman Vincent

Peale says about good preaching, and see how much of it applies to you, no matter what kind of talk you may be giving:

"It seems to me it's all very simple. You've got to have something to say, and you've got to believe what you say—you've got to be sincere about it. Then, stand up there and talk to the people in simple, everyday, United States English. Make the sentences short and crisp, succinct and snappy. Use some illustrative material that is germane to the lives of the people sitting out there. Pour into it whatever persuasiveness you can, and speak out in a clear, firm, resonant voice so they can hear what you say.

"I don't believe anybody has the right to go on any platform unless he sincerely believes everything he's going to say. If there's any phoniness or any doubt about it, that's sure to come through. And you've got to be enthusiastic. I don't believe there's any great difference between a sermon and an ordinary speech, except that the person in the pulpit has a 'thus-saith-the-Lord' kind of authority.

"If you're going to give a sermon, it has to be biblically based in some way," Dr. Peale continues. "But even a statement of the text a time or two will suffice for that. You don't have to go into elaborate detail. If you just quote Jesus, 'I've come that ye might have life and have it more abundantly,' that is really what it's all about.

"And a sermon should be very practical and tied down to your own experience. I myself promise them something in the first two or three sentences and then go on and tell them how the promise can be delivered. And then at the end, I [summarize] what I've told them and try to wrap it all up with an illustration. For example, I might be speaking on worry, and my first sentence might be, 'It is perfectly possible for you to get free of your worry.' Then I'd go on to say, 'I realize that this is a big order, but I happen to be a believer in the Bible, and in the thirty-fourth Psalm, the

194

fourth verse, it says, "I sought the Lord and He heard me and delivered me from all my fears." So *I'm* telling you that you can get rid of your fears, the Bible tells you that you can get rid of your fears—now, how do we go about doing it?' Then I'd explain one, two, three how you do it, with illustrations to make my point."

What Norman says about good preaching applies equally well to any kind of speaking. In effect, he's urging three things: Be personal, be practical, and be authoritative. I've pulled these and other principles together into what I call the five key lessons preachers can teach beginning speakers. Here they are:

Lesson 1:
Accept the authority of the platform.

No matter how often you may be told by me or Norman Vincent Peale or anybody else that you are capable of giving an effective speech, you may still find yourself assailed by deep doubts as you prepare to address your audience. Sometimes, lay people and even preachers speaking in a church pulpit feel the same way. There are always those lurking, often unspoken reservations, such as, "Who am I to be giving people advice . . . I haven't even had one course in speaking . . . I'm so imperfect, I don't see why anybody would even want to listen to me up here!"

Think for a moment: For some reason, you've been invited to give the speech. Apparently, somebody thinks you have something to say. So don't shy away from standing on the authority of the platform that's been offered to you—seize it and do your best to say something uplifting and significant to your listeners!

Lesson 2:
Serious topics can still be spiced with humor.

Neither sermons nor regular speeches have to be totally serious. In fact, some of the good preachers I know are quite adept at injecting a light remark or observation into an otherwise serious address. Joe Miller, for example, an insurance executive from Dallas who is also an ordained minister, was once delivering a sermon in a church that had an audio system with cordless microphones. The advantage of the system was that the speaker didn't have to worry about tripping over wires as he walked around behind the pulpit. But there was also a disadvantage—a tendency for the transmitter receiver equipment to pick up outside transmissions and broadcast them in the middle of the speech. Miller was deeply involved in explaining a difficult moral point when suddenly the sanctuary was filled with a local FM station commercial: "The Ajax Fertilizer Company is having a half-price sale—two bags for the price of one!"

Instead of ignoring the interruption or shaking his head piously, Miller responded, "Thank you, Lord, I will send my truck in the morning!"

Of course he got a laugh, and the congregation was even more attentive as he went back to his message.

There was a time, he said, when "I would have been very nervous, and something like that would have made me increase my talking speed to hurry through the interruption. But now I try to be more relaxed, and I've learned that an interruption like that can work as a real attention grabber. If you respond positively to the interruption, almost anything you say will be a little funny, and if you happen to hit on just the right thing, it might even be hilarious. It can be a plus to

196

have an interruption—sometimes I think I'd like to stage things like that."

So as long as you don't err on the side of flippancy in a serious address, you don't have to worry about using a few light or funny lines to brighten things up.

Lesson 3:
"Suffer little children . . ."

I've mentioned in another context that if children become disruptive in an ordinary speech, I might sometimes politely ask the parent to take them out. But in almost every situation—and especially those where your listeners have a strong family orientation—it's important to be sensitive and gentle with kids. If you're too heavy-handed in putting down children or their parents, you may succeed in shutting them up—but you may also alienate your audience.

There will most likely be a strong family tradition in many of the audiences you'll face, and it may even be helpful sometimes to think of your listeners as part of a church congregation—a position they may well occupy most Sunday mornings. In other words, remember that your audience's love for children may go back to Jesus' words in Matthew 19:14: "Suffer little children, and forbid them not, to come unto me; for of such is the kingdom of heaven."

So if you're going to try to get tough with kids or their parents, you have to be very careful. I usually prefer to attempt to correct situations involving kids with a little humor before I get stern with them. Joe Miller, for example, when confronted with a noisy child in church, might first say, "Well, at least somebody's listening!" Such a remark might get a laugh, and would also put the parent on notice that the child is being disruptive.

Also, I'm reminded of an observation by the Reverend Philip Clarke of the Park Avenue United Methodist Church in New York City. He was once asked after a sermon if a crying baby hadn't disconcerted him as he was speaking. But he replied, "Not at all. I can remember a time in this church when the congregation was so small that we didn't have any children. So I almost welcome hearing them during a service now!"

A sermon, in other words, is a serious undertaking, but it's important to keep in mind the compassion and love for other humans that usually underlie the message. A kind response to a child during an ordinary speech can also often do more for getting your point across than all the preparation you've done for the talk.

Lesson 4:
Avoid a tendency to be too abstract when you should be down-to-earth.

In some respects, this is just another way of saying, as Norman Vincent Peale has advised, that a good sermon or any speech has to be personal and practical.

I'm reminded of a friend of mine who was invited to give a lay sermon at his church in the Southwest. His topic was Christan love, and he worked long and hard analyzing the concept of love in the New Testament and comparing it with the idea of love held by Plato and other philosophers. The result was a sermon that would have made a great essay in a seminary course, but that managed to put half the congregation to sleep. What they wanted to hear was how they could learn to love more effectively themselves. What, they wondered, did the Bible say to them *personally* about expressing love to others? But my friend, unfortunately, never got around to that subject.

So when you're putting any speech together, do your homework and be certain you're on firm ground. Then focus on the concrete, practical applications of the principles you're discussing to the lives of your listeners. A good talk—and a good sermon, as well—cuts down into the heart; it doesn't get stuck up in the head.

Lesson 5:
Keep your speaking conversational.

A common mistake that beginning preachers make is to assume that giving a sermon requires a completely different oratorical style from other public speaking. They may think they have to model themselves after Billy Graham or Martin Luther King to do an adequate job; but that's not true at all. A person's style of delivering a sermon—and speaking to a secular group—should be much the same as the way he talks in conversation. Generally speaking, if a preacher keeps it natural and conversational, the message comes across much more effectively than if he tries to transform himself overnight into a flamboyant, hellfire-and-brimstone pulpiteer.

One man I know who used to live in Boston was asked by his church to deliver a sermon to the drunks and other down-and-outers at the Dover Street Mission in that city. This was the first sermon this fellow had ever given, and he decided that the only way he was going to inspire his listeners to change their way of living was to shout and scare the drink out of them.

Unfortunately, the style he chose was completely different from his own reserved personality. He could do a good job delivering a low-key talk in a conversational tone of voice. But he sounded like a caricature of the old-time evangelist Billy Sunday when he stood up before his inebriated audience that evening. He shouted and railed at them in an abrasive, accusatory way, but all he succeeded in doing was to turn them completely off.

Don't fall into this trap in your public speaking. Just be yourself up there on the platform, and you'll find you're much more convincing. Also, your listeners will be much more inclined to accept what you're saying as authoritative and worth applying in their own lives.

A sermon is a special kind of speech with special requirements. To be a good preacher takes a great deal of training and experience—and more than a casual dose of inspiration and conviction. But I'm convinced, despite all the obvious differences, that there are a lot of similarities between good preaching and good secular speaking. Perhaps you can learn a great deal not only about the meaning of life but also about communicating effectively to any audience if you just visit your local church occasionally or tune in on a good TV preacher every now and then.

CHAPTER SIXTEEN

⚜ ⚜ ⚜

Talking on the Tube

I f you ever become a leader in anything, the odds will greatly increase that you could be asked to speak on your field of expertise to a radio or television audience. You may have become involved in helping to settle refugees in this country. You may become active in the PTA or the Chamber of Commerce. Or you may be the best at doing needlework in your community. Or you may have established yourself as a top retailer or salesman. Whatever your claim to fame, you might well be called on to participate in an interview over the airwaves—and that will require some special public speaking skills.

In most speeches, you have a little time to unwind

before an audience. You can ease gradually into your topic, and although there may be some time constraints, they will probably be relatively loose. Or as your host may say to you, "Our speakers *usually* talk *about* forty-five minutes."

But on radio and television, the rules change dramatically. Time becomes much more valuable, and if you drift off into an irrelevancy for even a sentence or two, you're likely to find the interviewer interrupting you to try to get you back on the track. I've known individuals who could deliver a beautiful thirty- or forty-minute address, but who fell apart when they looked into a TV camera or radio microphone because they were unable to make the transition to this kind of public speaking.

As with any other speaking skill, talking really well on radio or television takes practice. But you can start right out doing at least an adequate job if you keep in mind these eight fundamental principles, which have guided me during the decades I've spent doing interviews and being interviewed:

1. Keep your answers short and to the point.

Talking on a radio or television interview is different from any other speaking because of the tremendous time pressure you'll be under. This kind of speaking is not like a lecture, and it's not like ordinary conversation. When you're asked the first question—a question, by the way, that may be vague or downright silly because the interviewer himself may not be particularly skilled or experienced—you have to get off the starting blocks fast. There's no time for much of an introduction. You might say some pleasantry in a short phrase or sentence—perhaps something about how happy you are to be on the program or to be talking to the interviewer. But you should then immediately go to the most concrete, specific point you can think of in response to the question you've been asked. If you stick to vague abstractions in your answer, you're going to come across as a total bore.

Above all, get their *attention*. For example, "In our town *right now* there is a theft happening every three minutes. Is your car or home safe?"

I think it's a good idea in your preparation for this sort of appearance to spend some time boiling down your thoughts and potential answers to three or four simple, specific ideas. Try to anticipate the questions you may be asked and then jot down a few specific points you might use to respond to the questions. If you spend only ten to fifteen minutes for this anticipation process, you'll probably be able to come up with answers to at least eighty percent of the questions you'll be asked.

But if you fail to prepare and do begin to get long-winded and ramble off onto some irrelevant issue, I hope the situation doesn't get as bad as it did with me one time when I was conducting a "Man in the Street" radio interview in San Diego. I had learned from doing this sort of interview that one of the most difficult things for an interviewer is to cut off a talkative, dull speaker without making him or the audience angry. In most cases, the interviewer can employ a number of clever tricks to stop things. But I ran into some special difficulties with this particular subject.

It was raining, and no one was on the street that day, and I was getting desperate to find someone to get on the air for my program. The interview was scheduled to be aired live, and I was standing there all alone! The red light flashed. I was on the air.

Suddenly a man walked out of a restaurant nearby. I immediately ran over and collared him for an interview. Just after I asked him who he was, though, I saw that he was drunk. He was soon slurring his words, propping himself up against me, and mumbling a series of unintelligible replies that made it impossible even to fake a good interview.

So I told him, "Well, it's been nice talking to you, and I want to thank you on behalf of our listeners. But it's obvious you're having such a good time you don't want to waste any more time with us. . . . "

As I turned to walk away, he grabbed my arm roughly and shouted, "You can't ditch me like that! Who'n hell do you think you are?" Then he started *really* swearing at me.

The more I tried to free myself and my microphone from his grasp, the more this fellow seemed to tie me up in his arms. I could almost hear the seconds ticking way, and I knew the audience must be thinking they had tuned into the craziest program in town.

As a last resort, I did something I had never done before and have never done since—I hit him right in the mouth with my fist! He fell to the ground and so did my microphone, but at least I had regained control of the situation. I quickly picked up the mike and immediately apologized to my audience:

"I feel any guest I invite into your home on this program is my problem," I told them. "And if he is profaning your family with obscene language, any action of mine should be justified under the circumstances because I have to protect you. So for your information, I want you to know I had to hit him. . . . Of course I *did* notice first that he's smaller than I am."

Now this dramatic encounter was rather extreme. I seriously doubt that you'll ever have to worry about someone slugging you if you get off the track in any interviews you do. But the basic lesson is the same: You'll frustrate your interviewer and come across as a bore on radio or TV if you fail to keep your responses succinct and to the point.

2. Don't limit your answers to a "yes" or "no."

This principle is the other side of the coin from the one we just discussed. It's true that you should keep your answers short and to the point, but they shouldn't be so short that your interviewer has to strain to get anything out of you. You're the one being interviewed, so you should do most of the talking. But be conversational. You're not making a speech. Be as normal as you can without long stories or too many statistics. The interviewer may get frustrated if he senses that getting information out of you is like pulling teeth. On the other hand, if you go on too long, you'll risk drifting off into topics that the interviewer didn't ask you about and may not be interested in discussing.

3. Speak in simple, everyday language.

This is a principle of delivering any speech that is especially important when you're speaking on radio or TV. The key to good radio or television is the simple, direct message—whether that message is coming across in a commercial, situation comedy, or interview. And you can't keep things simple if you're reeling off complex words that only a minute percentage of your audience understands. Remember that the audience you are reaching may total millions—but they are sitting in groups of two or three. So speak in the same way you would in someone's living room with only two people present.

I love to play with words, and I'm frequently tempted to use some of the long, resonant ones I come across in my reading when I speak to an audience. Just recently, I was talking about effective salesmanship, and I said something about pulling out "every technique from your sales armamentarium." Now, that word "armamentarium" can't be found in many of the smaller, abridged dictionaries most people use. You have to go to the big, complete ones to find it means "the total store of available resources" or "the equipment used in an activity or profession."

So even though "armamentarium" may have been a fun word for me to use, it actually worked against good communication. And if you try to display your Howard Cosell verbal pyrotechnics during a radio or television program, you're going to be committing a much worse sin than you will in an ordinary speech. *Remember:* The time constraints in the electronic media dictate quick, clear communication. Anything that interferes with this goal, such as the use of complex, obscure words, will seriously hinder your effectiveness as a speaker.

4. Formulate a few slogans and repeat them during the interview.

When you're speaking for a short time on radio or TV, you have to assume that your listeners will only listen to a portion of what you're saying. And unless you choose your words very carefully, they're likely to forget quickly everything they have heard.

So I would suggest that you follow a couple of practices that advertising copywriters use when they're writing copy for commercials or billboards: Try to phrase your major points in a couple of catchy slogans, and then repeat those slogans several times in the context of your answers. In this way, if your listeners catch only a portion of your interview, they'll at least be more likely to hear you make your major points—and they'll be more likely to remember those points because you've presented them in a memorable way. For instance, when I'm trying to arouse my audience to the problem of apathy in a drug abuse crusade, I say over and over, "Unfortunately, the American public has two speeds—panic and apathy."

One man who is a master of the memorable turn of phrase is my friend, the Reverend Dr. Robert Schuller, of the "Hour of Power" religious TV program. He's a great positive thinker, and he likes to stress the benefits of positive thinking in as many different ways as he can. So he has come up with an award for those who have overcome difficulties in life which he calls the "Turn Your Scars into Stars Award." The rhyme and alliteration in this phrase make it easy to remember, and the point is so simple and clear it can't be missed: This is an award for those who have turned tragedies into triumphs, or failures into successes. I feel flattered that I am one of the recipients.

The principle of repeating your key points in a catchy way applies no matter what you're trying to impress on your audience: Perhaps you want to promote an organization you represent, or a piece of important consumer information you've discovered, or a book you've written.

Whatever your main reason for being on the program, be sure that you identify it clearly in your mind before the interview and try to express it in an interesting way. Then if you repeat your key point several times while you're on the air, the chances are you'll get your message across to the widest possible audience.

5. Be opinionated.

Interviewers don't want equivocal, wishy-washy speakers on their programs. If they ask you to participate, they expect you to take a strong position and defend it. If you feel you can't take a strong position on the topic under discussion, then you probably shouldn't try to communicate with a radio or TV audience.

For example, if you've been asked to do a program on school busing, and you're known to be opposed to it, you shouldn't get on the air and say, "Well, I know there are many arguments both pro and con, and I can see the merits on both sides, but I'm inclined to think busing probably shouldn't be allowed in this city—though I'm certainly willing to change my position if somebody comes along with a convincing argument!"

That approach might work in a lengthy speech, where you can explain and qualify during thirty or forty minutes behind a podium. But it won't work on the electronic media. When asked what you think about busing, you've got to say, "No, busing should never be allowed in this city!" Or if you really want to become the darling of the radio and TV talk shows, you might say, "Anybody who tries to bus my child will get a punch right in the schnozolla!'' The reaction of the listeners at home to such a statement will probably be "Holy smoke!" And that's the reaction your interviewer is looking for.

Some people are just not constitutionally suited to take such a strong stand. They want to ease into their positions on various issues with all sorts of reservations and qualifications. But you have to make up your mind to overcome these cautious tendencies if you want to make a successful impact on the air.

6. Be as personal as possible.

We're in the age of the public confessional on radio and TV talk shows, and if you've been asked to speak on a topic that involves personal or intimate experiences you've had, your interviewer and your audience will expect you to deliver the goods. If you watch closely to see which celebrities are the most popular on the national talk shows, you'll notice it's those who talk about the startling, the bizarre, the revelatory, and the personal confession. It's the man who says, "Yes, this was the seventh girl I've married in five years," and then who is willing to go on and talk about his unusual love life.

But I don't want to give you the wrong impression on this point. It may be that the topic you've been asked to discuss doesn't involve anything particularly confessional, and in any case a description of the color of the underwear you use may not be relevant. But there's a personal side to almost every topic you can talk about, and the more personal anecdotes and illustrations you can inject to make your points, the more effectively you'll be able to communicate on radio and TV.

7. Be animated and enthusiastic.

In ordinary conversation—as well as in an ordinary speech—there are periods in your talking when your voice becomes somewhat flat and unemotional. Often, toning down your delivery this way can enhance the impact of your speech by highlighting those moments when your voice rises to a crescendo to make a strong point.

But on short radio and television appearances, you don't have the luxury of allowing yourself to slip into those "dead" moments. You've got to keep "up" and enthusiastic during most of your presentation, or your listeners may well decide you're as bored with what you're saying as they are.

So be prepared to increase the pace of your speaking and put plenty of life and emphasis into your responses as the interviewer questions you. When you're on television, don't be afraid to gesture and use animated facial expressions *so long as they are natural to you*. Smile every now and then, too. There's nothing I dislike more than a person sitting before a TV camera with a deadpan expression, an immobile body, and a listless monotone of a delivery. I quickly tune out what he's saying—unless the topic is inherently so interesting to me that I'm willing to overlook his dull manner of presenting his views.

But I should mention, in a word of caution, that your smiling and animation must be appropriate. It's as bad and distracting to allow your body to jerk and jump around for no good reason as it is to keep as still as concrete. Perhaps the worst kind of inappropriate animation is the phony, out-of-place smile. I can recall one talk-show host, who shall go unnamed, who was interviewing a policeman on the problem of child pornography and prostitution. This subject is one of the most distasteful and sickening that you

210

can find these days, and as far as I can tell, there's no way to make light of it. Yet this host spent the entire twenty minutes of the interview with a smile plastered on his face. I know one viewer who got so angry at the host's insensitivity that he actually began yelling at the television image for this display of bad taste.

So pump yourself up before you go on the air, and keep the pitch of your delivery higher and more enthusiastic than you might normally try to sustain for the duration of the show. But always keep your mind on what's being discussed and fit those animated reactions of yours to each question and situation so that your delivery will come across as perfectly appropriate and natural. Keep your chin up to avoid unflattering lines. Don't slump into your chair. And keep an unfailing eye-to-eye contact with your host.

8. Never use notes on TV.

You'll notice I've limited this tip to TV. There's generally no problem with carrying a few notes to a radio studio, or using them if you're being interviewed for the radio over a telephone hook-up at your home (which is a very common technique for smaller stations). The only possible difficulty with using notes on radio is that you might have a tendency to become so absorbed in flipping through them that you forget to listen to the questions being put to you by your interviewer.

But notes are deadly for a TV appearance because the camera sees all. The format for most talk shows is to have both the interviewer and the guest seated in easy chairs in full view of the cameras and studio audience. So if you have notes with you, it will be impossible to hide them. One

211

difficulty with this is you'll tend to look as though you're really not completely on top of your material if you can't speak right off the top of your head. Also, as I just pointed out, eye contact with your host and with the camera is important in effective television speaking, and that becomes very difficult if you're constantly looking down to refer to your notes. The only exception would be if you were quoting a Gallup poll or other "hard-fact" reference.

So I would advise you to make a few notes ahead of time, boil them down to the three or four key points you want to make, attach a key word to each of those points for easy recall, and then memorize those major words or themes. Go over several times, out loud, the questions you expect you'll be asked on the program and the answers you expect to give. Refer to your notes during these practice sessions if you need them to boost your memory. But then put them into your pocket and don't take them out when you walk onto the TV set. You'll probably find your first television appearance to be nerve-racking because you won't be exactly sure how you'll perform. But after you've done it once and seen it's not as bad as you thought, you'll probably become quite comfortable with the television format.

These are the barest fundamentals for effective radio and television speaking, but I think if you take them seriously as you prepare for your appearance, you'll find you can do at least an acceptable job—and you may even be excellent. But don't let one or two successes make you complacent! Most amateur speakers don't do enough speaking on the electronic media to ever be able to let their guards down. I've known many people who make occasional appearances on radio and television, and after they've done one fine job, they think they're naturals at this sort of thing and success should be automatic. But it's not. Usually, this complacent attitude tempts the speaker to skimp on his preparation in some way. He may not try to anticipate the questions he'll be asked; or he may not boil his responses down to the simplest and most colorful phrasing he can formulate; or he may neglect to "pump himself" up to be especially animated and enthusiastic.

A failure to prepare and practice radio and television presentations has the same deflating effect as failing to prepare for any kind of speech: The words don't come fluently, the organization is loose and confusing, and the message doesn't get communicated. But if you take your radio and television appearances as seriously as any other speech you're invited to deliver, you'll discover you can do just as well on the air as in any other public speaking forum.

CHAPTER SEVENTEEN

⚜ ⚜ ⚜

From
Private Person
to Perry Mason

W e've already taken a close look at what preachers can contribute to the beginner's knowledge of public speaking. But there's another group of specialists who exercise their vocal cords for a living at least as much as the clergy—and who can give us a somewhat different perspective on techniques for addressing and persuading audiences. I'm referring to lawyers, and especially trial lawyers, the real-life "Perry Masons" of our day.

An attorney who is highly qualified to instruct us on this point is my good friend, the great trial lawyer and author, Louis Nizer. Nizer, who has written *My Life In Court, The Jury Returns, Thinking On Your Feet,* and many other books on his courtroom exploits, suggests first of all that amateur speakers keep in mind three basic principles that he believes apply to *all* effective public speaking, both in and outside the courtroom.

"First," he says, "the more one talks to audiences, the easier it is. The natural fright of making an address diminishes in proportion to the number of times you do it. After a while, you're not distracted by movements and people talking to one another. You're in control of the situation. The highest form of skill in public speaking is when you can not only not be bothered by the faces and actions of your audience, but also observe and evaluate them. If they're perplexed, their foreheads will show creases, and you'll know you have to repeat or explain yourself more thoroughly."

So wherever you're talking, the more you can read an audience's reactions and then respond to the way they're accepting your message, the more effective you'll be. As an example, he says, "If I were talking about democracy, I might say, 'The principle that validates democracy is a scientific principle: As you multiply judgments, you diminish the errors.' But as I make that statement, I may look at you and see you screw up your eyes, to indicate you don't understand. So I stop and repeat myself slowly and perhaps explain in more detail: 'Two heads are better than one, and a hundred are better than ten. That's the principle of democracy and that's the reason I'd rather trust 200 million Americans on the question of right or wrong than I would the ten most brilliant people in the world.' Now that's real public speaking, when you're not just talking, but talking *to your audience*."

The second general principle of public speaking that Nizer follows is that "no speech should be read." That sounds rather familiar, doesn't it? In case you've picked this book up and started reading in the middle, I'd suggest you flip back to Chapter Ten, where I treat this principle in some detail.

But Nizer goes even further than I do: "If you want to be really proficient, your speech should be delivered without looking at a note," he says. "Everybody has a good memory and a bad memory. It's all in concentration. If you concentrate on anything, you have a good memory. If you don't, you're an absentminded fellow. Proof? Suppose you go to a motion picture show. It's a fascinating feature, and you go home and tell your wife every scene. Then you go to a cocktail party and get introduced to the same fellow three times, but you never do catch his name.

"My own preparation for any kind of talk is that I walk up and down a room and in my own mind I deliver the talk orally. I never write it out. I walk up and down for miles in my house. If one paragraph doesn't flow naturally into another, I forget it because I know it's a bad paragraph. An audience follows you by anticipation. If I have trouble when I construct a speech and always forget what my next point is going to be, I know it's the wrong point."

Louis Nizer prefers relying on his memory and staying away from all notes, in part because he believes there's too much of a temptation to read parts of your speech if you're using notes. And he says, "The rhythm of communicating orally is completely different from reading something. Ninety-seven percent of all speeches are read, and that's the reason they are dull."

The lawyer's third basic principle of effective speaking is that "without an original thought no speech is good." He says that the best speeches are those that are artfully constructed around a unique, creative idea. But even if you don't have an original concept, he says, you can do some research and deliver a good speech by "putting some information before the audience that they don't know. That's why *everybody* can make a good speech in this sense. If a person knows his subject—insurance, painting a house, auto construction—and follows some basic public speaking rules, he can give a fascinating speech."

These are the three fundamental principles that Attorney Louis Nizer keeps in mind for all his public speaking appearances. But what *specific* guidelines does he derive from his courtroom experience? Nizer offers two court-related tips for successfully persuading an audience:

1. Organize your facts simply and clearly.

"The hardest thing to do in any law office is to find clarity and lucidity," he says. "I can get ten brilliant lawyers for any one who can write [or speak] clearly, without any chance of ambiguity. The ambiguities flow with every sentence—such things as using the word 'they' when it's not clear whether the speaker is referring to the plaintiffs or defendants."

2. Decide how to tip the scales of justice slightly in your favor.

"We all have a sense of right or wrong," Nizer explains. "The art of persuasion in court is to make that scale of justice tip just a little bit, but not overwhelmingly, in your favor. Legal decisions are based on a preponderance, not a unanimity, of the evidence. When you or I get a set of facts, we know inherently, through an innate moral sense, whether one side or the other is right. Indeed, judges admit that they apply the law *after* they have reached an opinion. Justice [Benjamin] Cardozo was a master at that. He said the judicial process involved deciding first who was right, and then justifying [that decision] with law."

The best way to "tip the scales of justice" toward your side of an argument is to "create an atmosphere in the courtroom that you are right, and after that any disputes on the law begin to fall your way," he advises. Another way of approaching any speech by using this principle would be to gather all your facts together and then sit down and ask yourself, "Why am I right?" Pick those facts that provide the strongest support for the justice of your position, and stress them over and over again in your talk—to create that "courtroom atmosphere" in your favor, which Nizer refers to.

Louis Nizer has tested this "tip the scales of justice" technique throughout his career in the courtroom, and he's found it to be one of the more fundamental and valid principles of his practice. "I *have* made tests of this," he stresses, "and I believe no legal brief is good unless your twelve-year-old daughter can understand it when she reads it—*and* unless she thinks you're right!" He says he'll sometimes draft a legal brief and have a lay person read it; and then he'll add one fact and submit the brief again. "The whole opinion of my case will change if I omit that one fact from the brief," he says.

As an example of how this principle works in an actual courtroom situation, he cites his experience in the Freuhauf labor case: "That case involved a law—a draconian law—which said that, with no qualifications, an officer of a company could not give a loan to a labor leader. Freuhauf

219

was indicted for having given a loan of several hundred thousand dollars to Beck, a labor leader.

"Now, this case looked open-and-shut for the government. The fact that the money was given as a loan was conceded. It didn't matter if it was paid with sufficiently high interest—it was illegal. But the jury acquitted Freuhauf, and it did so on the basis of one fact, which I thought tipped the scales of persuasion. Curiously enough, the prosecutor in the case, an able fellow, was eager to have that fact in the case. He thought it showed more transactions between Freuhauf and the labor leader. And of course, I wanted it in there too.

"Here's that key fact: At one point there was a raid on Freuhauf's company by some stockbrokers, and he needed money desperately to buy up some of his own stock to protect himself. So he went to the labor leader, Beck, and Beck arranged for a loan in a bank. He just used his influence with the bank, but didn't violate any law. As a result, Freuhauf was able to buy up a lot of his stock and save his business.

"Subsequently, Beck had a disaster in real estate in San Francisco, and he needed a loan to save his real estate. So he went to Freuhauf and said, 'I'd like you to help me out.' This request had nothing to do with labor matters. We showed in court that all the labor contracts were the same as before, and no preferences were shown to anybody. As I said to the jury, Freuhauf would have been a heel to say he couldn't do it. So Freuhauf gave Beck the loan, which was eventually paid back in full. It was a matter of one man doing another a favor—how could Freuhauf refuse a man who had helped him out?"

Nizer knew that the information about that first loan, from Beck to Freuhauf, was probably irrelevant to the present case, and the prosecutor could have kept it out through an objection. But the prosecutor chose not to, and Nizer was equally eager to keep the testimony in about that initial loan to create the atmosphere of one man innocently returning a favor he owed to another. "If you leave that fact out—if you just say there was one loan to so-and-so—you're convicted," the lawyer explains.

As a result of the atmosphere that Nizer created in the courtroom—the tipping of the scales of justice slightly in his client's favor—Freuhauf was acquitted. The jury in effect modified the statutory law by deciding that if a loan has nothing to do with labor dealing, it's all right.

Now, I certainly don't expect to turn you into a Louis Nizer, F. Lee Bailey or Clarence Darrow just by having you read this book. But I do believe that if you keep some of these guidelines in mind as you prepare your speeches, you may very well find you can convince almost any audience of your position. The principles of public speaking—with the modifications Louis Nizer has suggested in this chapter—are basically the same in the courtroom and behind the podium at your local Rotary Club. So don't be surprised if you discover there really are a few traits of Perry Mason in your very private personality!

CHAPTER EIGHTEEN

☘ ☘ ☘

Wars of
Words

W e've already discussed in great detail how to persuade people, both in the average auditorium and in the courtroom. But there's another situation you may very well encounter where you'll have to employ a slightly different kind of convincing argument—the head-to-head debate.

The classic prototype of this type of confrontation would be the formal high school or college debate, where the roles of those representing the opposing sides are highly stylized and fixed by certain rules about rebuttals and other stages of the presentation. But I'm not talking about this kind of competition. The kind of debate I'm referring to is much less formal—but may well be just as intense. You may find yourself in a public argument at a P.T.A. meeting; at a panel discussion on some controversial issue like abortion or real estate zoning; or on a radio or TV program where several other people are being interviewed with you.

You may be invited to speak in an environment where you know beforehand that there are going to be some disagreements, or you may just find yourself embroiled in an argument unexpectedly during an otherwise harmonious meeting. In any case, there are a number of techniques you can use to defend yourself and sway your listeners during these "wars of words." And that's the skill I want to introduce you to now.

If I'm expecting to face a debate situation, I rely on three resources to get successfully through the challenge.

First of all, I do some *extra-intensive preparation and research*. You've probably noticed I haven't put much emphasis in this book on research, in the sense of gathering a great many facts and figures. I certainly always believe in thorough preparation by organizing your speech, going over and over transitions, and practicing your delivery. But hard-core research has taken a back seat because I believe it's not usually the most important element in an effective talk.

In a debate, though, the equation for effective speaking changes. You have to have plenty of facts to bolster your arguments and to meet your opponent's counter-thrusts. So I would suggest that you plan on trying to learn at least five times as much about your subject as you would ordinarily try to learn.

My second major resource—which is actually a direct outgrowth of the first—is that I always gather an *arsenal of outside authority*, instead of relying primarily on my own personal opinions and experiences. Again, as you can see, this principle diverges from the approach I've suggested you follow in giving most other speeches. References to your personal experiences and opinions are essential to fascinating public speaking in most circumstances. But too much reliance on the personal approach can actually harm your effectiveness in a debate.

For example, if you use a reference to something you and your spouse have discovered in your family life as a supposedly definitive illustration in a debate on child-rearing, you're on thin ice. The reason? Your opponent will probably attack you right at that point by demanding, "Can't you offer anything other than an isolated personal anecdote to support your position?" If you can't come up with any facts or studies, you'll appear to be either poorly prepared or the unfortunate advocate of an extremely weak side of the argument.

Some types of outside authority that debaters often use to good advantage are incontrovertible studies and surveys (e.g., the Gallup Poll or findings by the Bureau of Labor Statistics); historical antecedents (e.g., "opening our nation's doors to Far Eastern refugees can strengthen local communities, as is evidenced by the experience of the Yorkville section of Manhattan in 1976 . . ."); and generalizations based on the clear perceptions of the audience (e.g., "everyone here knows that this very month is the biggest time during the entire year for catching fish off this coast . . . ").

The third and final resource I rely on in a debate is that I always make sure I *prepare both sides of the issue equally well.* My rationale in doing this two-pronged preparation is that I know if I can learn my opponent's argument as well as he knows it, I'll be able to counter his attacks more competently.

I was especially relieved I had prepared both sides of the issue for a debate I was invited to participate in on television in Canada a few years ago. But the reason for my relief was somewhat different from what you might expect.

I thought that I had been asked to take the positive side of the question, "Are children today over-privileged?" In other words, I was supposed to argue that kids today *are* over-privileged. But when I walked out on the stage in front of those live TV cameras on a coast-to-coast Canadian station, I heard the host introducing me as the speaker who would be carrying the banner for the *negative* side of the question.

I had obviously been given the wrong information, but there was nothing I could do about that now. The speaker for the "positive" always begins the debate. I realized the opening remarks would take about five minutes and that meant I had five minutes to reorganize my thinking and formulate a convincing presentation to show that contemporary kids are really underprivileged.

Fortunately, I had followed the advice I've just given you and had thoroughly studied both sides of the question. So I knew all the strong points of the negative approach to the question. All that remained was for me to marshal those facts and authorities into a convincing piece of persuasion.

When the other speaker finished his five-minute introduction, I had just finished readjusting my thought processes. As he sat down, I stood up and began, "My opponent argues that the child of today is over-privileged because he is given everything, and I thoroughly agree with that statement. But that is the core of my argument against his being over-privileged: Because he is given everything, he's actually *under*privileged. He is not able to define his own goals, to build up his own defense mechanisms, or to face adversity—because he is given everything. He has the worst possible disadvantage because he has never learned what it means to scramble for something. . . . "

I made it through my initial presentation all right and was really able to shine in my rebuttal, which is usually my strong point in a debate. And according to the meter evaluating audience applause on the show, I won the debate. Actually, it's not so surprising that I could do a successful job under these circumstances, because both sides of the issue had been studied in depth and organized clearly and logically in advance.

These, then, are the distinctive preparation techniques you should keep in mind if you think you may get embroiled in a debate. But before we leave this subject, I should mention that the stress I've been putting on gathering solid facts and research doesn't mean that your argumentative speaking should be dull, cold, or totally impersonal. Many debaters lose because they fail to bring their facts to life. So get a good stack of authorities for your debate, but then step back and ask yourself, "How can I get my audience excited about all this material?" If you can get your listeners interested and involved in what you're saying, you'll be much more likely to encourage them to become sympathetic to your side of the issue.

CHAPTER NINETEEN

♣ ♣ ♣

Speaking of
Business . . .

The final specialized speaking technique I want to discuss with you is, in some respects, the most important of all. I'm referring to giving reports, sales presentations, and other talks in a business environment.

If you're going to get ahead in business, it's essential that you know how to communicate easily and clearly to your peers, bosses, and prospective clients. But I find that, far too often, people fall apart when they stand up to say something to their business colleagues—and that's a real shame, because many times these ineffectual speakers are the ones who have the most to say.

If you've learned some of the basics of giving a talk

under the variety of circumstances we've already discussed, you'll find you're much more at ease when you get up to make a presentation in an office or boardroom. But there are some special techniques and devices you should be aware of if you want to turn in a truly superior performance.

First of all, don't begin a business report with a joke! This doesn't mean that you shouldn't be open to some light remarks or an occasional humorous observation after you get rolling in presenting your report. But it's too big a chance to take, to try to succeed with an initial joke and at the same time convince your listeners you're a person worth taking seriously. After all, business is rooted in profits, and you're up there to show your audience how they can make money. Believe me, they're not as interested in laughing as they are in making a buck, so keep first things first!

In a similar vein, I'm reminded of reactions I've heard to politicians like Senator Robert Dole and Adlai Stevenson when they were running for high office. Both were witty men, but a typical reaction to them would be, "He's funny, but I don't want a guy in the White House telling jokes!" There may be times for a free-wheeling emphasis on humor in public speaking, but Presidential campaigns and serious business discussions are not among them.

With this principle in mind, then, let's go directly to the heart of the business reports and other presentations you'll be giving. The two key areas that make business speeches distinctive are the use of slides or other visual aids and the special preparation of notes that can be used smoothly with these props. To provide us with some observations and illustrations in this area, I've asked for contributions from two experts—James Vaughan, President of Related Designs, Inc. in New York City, and Joe Miller, the head of the McNeil/Miller Insurance Agency in Dallas.

Vaughan, who is a designer with an acute sense of the impact of visual aids in business meetings, has made hundreds of slide and graphic presentations to executives from major corporations like Citibank and Steelcase. Before he even walks into a business office, however, he always goes through a preliminary preparation routine which includes, above all, "doing my homework so thoroughly that I expect to have plenty of information at my disposal which will never be used in my presentation, I typically present only fifty to sixty percent of what I'm ready to give."

He also does a last-minute check on the way he looks, primarily because businessmen can be among the most demanding and critical of a speaker's appearance. "I don't over- or under-dress," Vaughan says. "Anything that draws attention to yourself should be left out—no big jewelry or bright colors. Always be sure your fly is zipped and your shoes shined. Also, the last thing you should do before you walk before a group is to check yourself in the mirror—especially in bad or windy weather—just to be certain everything is on straight."

In the same situation, a woman will want to wear an outfit appropriate for the occasion and to make a last-minute check in the mirror on her hair and make-up and see that her seams are straight.

Since he frequently takes slides, graphs, or other graphic material up to the podium, James Vaughan pays particular attention to the *way* he carries these things. "I try to appear relaxed and in control of all my visual aids," he says. "If you look like a garbage collector, with items spilling out of each arm, you automatically lose impact in your talk. I would recommend buying some professional-looking containers, such as a large black zipper case with handles for large boards, graphs, and charts. And if you tape things together, be sure you practice putting them together smoothly before you give your speech. Otherwise, you'll find yourself trying to cram boards into too-small packages or having to carry them separately when you leave, and this makes you look disorganized. Try to leave as compactly as you arrived."

Once you get into the room where you're making your presentation, Vaughan says, it's very important to be certain that the *scale* of your visual aids is adjusted to the number of people in your audience. For example, you'll probably want smaller graphs and photographs if you're talking to only ten people than if you're addressing fifty or a hundred.

As far as slides are concerned, they should be projected onto a screen or wall that's high enough so that no heads block off the picture. "Also, there's a fine line between producing something too sophisticated, which could overpower the audience or could give you technical problems in keeping control of the presentation; and creating something so 'rinky-dink' that you appear to be poorly prepared," James Vaughan says.

He advises that you check and double-check the arrangement of your slides, and go through the entire program with the projector just prior to your presentation to be sure that everything is in order. "If a slide comes through upside down, that destroys the momentum of your talk," he explains. It could also destroy a serious mood.

Another important principle in doing a slide presentation at a business gathering is to "keep things moving," he says. "Television has given almost everyone a shorter attention span these days, so don't let any picture linger before the eyes of your listeners for too long, or you'll lose them."

But just in case you happen to move too quickly for any of the people in your audience, he suggests using a projector with a device that allows you to back up the previous slide for extra viewing and explanation. As an example of the kind of pace he uses, he says he recently went through a presentation of thirty-nine slides in about seven minutes—an average viewing time of only about eleven seconds per slide.

He also tries to arrange his slides in such an order that they tell an interesting story, which moves logically from one point to another. For example, if he were discussing the merits of a certain building in a large city, he might start out with a picture of the street sign, to show exactly where the building was located. Next, he might include a couple of broad shots of the neighborhood to illustrate the general setting for the property. He also tries to retain some elements of surprise in his presentation so that he can pique his listeners' curiosity about what's coming next. For example, he might show a building floor by floor, so that the viewer gets the impression he's exploring the premises along with the speaker. And he might try dropping little anticipatory hints, such as "You'll see that the water damage on this ceiling is nothing compared with what I'm going to show you next."

But slides aren't the only visual aids available for you to use in a business report, and, in fact, Vaughan recommends that you not rely solely on slides or any other single graphic prop. "It's possible to tell a business story in many different ways, and the more means you use, the more people you're likely to reach," he says. "Some types of visual media get through to some people but leave others cold. So try at least two or three methods in presenting your talk."

Some people, for example, may respond more readily

to cardboard graphs and charts than they do to photographs or slides. So if your talk lends itself to both methods, you should include both. Insurance man Joe Miller, who has achieved the Million Dollar Round Table for many years in sales, often uses graphs to make his points, and he stresses that organization and preparation are as important with this method of presentation as with slides. Miller, whom we've already heard from on the subject of giving lay sermons, says he frequently uses transparent overlays on his graphs when he has several trends he's trying to plot. In this way, he can control the pace at which his audience receives his information.

"I might plot three items—premium, cash value, and interest rate—on a certain type of insurance policy," Miller says. "But I can build up to them gradually, one step at a time, if I use overlays. So the graph itself might contain the line showing the premium. The first overlay might show the cash values. And the second overlay would indicate the interest rate. This method enables me to talk about one point at a time, without confusing the issue by confronting my audience with all the graph's lines at once. Also, if I present my talk in gradual visual steps this way, I'm more sure the listeners are concentrating on what I'm talking about and not on one of the items I haven't yet reached."

Finally, Miller has a technique for preparing his notes for a business report which I think you'll find helpful. Because he, like James Vaughan, often uses graphic aids during his talks, he frequently finds he has to look up to point to certain items on his charts or slides. To facilitate this process, he always stands next to the spot where the graph is placed or the slide is being projected—and that may require his having a remote control device for the slide projector. "I want people to be looking at me as well as at the visual aids," he explains, "and that means I have to

234

stand close to their line of vision as they view the graphic devices I've chosen."

But the main problem with looking up at the visual aids and then back to his notes in these presentations is that it's very easy for him to lose his place in his notes. So he has devised a scheme for highlighting his notes with colored pens to make it easier to keep his presentation going smoothly.

He says he usually employs two bright colors—one to underline key points or statements he may want to emphasize or repeat several times and another to highlight his transitions from one major point to the next. "I may have three key points I plan to make in my presentation, and they would be numbered Roman numeral I and II and III," he explains. "If I'm in transition from II to III, I would underline the transition in my notes in a bright color. Then I can keep my eye contact with my audience right up to the point when I make that transition and still be able to go back to the proper spot in my notes by looking for the appropriate transition color. If I don't have that transition highlighted, I'll have to scan my notes to find where I am, and that may delay the smooth flow of my presentation. How many times have you been reading a book, been interrupted, looked up, and then been forced to scan several lines to find out where you were when you stopped reading? Speakers face the same problem if they frequently look up from their notes, and highlighting can help you avoid this problem."

Frankly, I think this approach to preparing your notes could be helpful in almost any kind of speaking situation. But in a business presentation, where you're much more likely to have to look up to point to graphic props, look at the audience, or answer questions, some technique like this becomes even more important to keep things going smoothly.

Good public speaking in a business setting may be more important to your future than any other kind of public address because those businessmen listening to you may well have the power to decide your future with the company or stack the odds in favor of your securing a lucrative contract. Your audience will be listening not only to what you say; they will also be listening and looking to evaluate the way you say it. Your style of presentation will tell them a great many things about your personality and abilities: Are you well-organized? Articulate? Can you simplify difficult concepts or do you tend to get confused by complexity? Do you work hard to prepare speaking tasks that are assigned to you?

There are many other things that might be said about making a business speech, but the main things we're concerned with in this book are the basics. If you want more detailed information about how to deliver a business talk, there are many courses and seminars you can take on this subject. But no matter how much more you learn about business speaking techniques, I would suggest you always keep some of the fundamental points that have been made in this chapter in the forefront of your mind: Be prepared. Keep it moving. Make it clear. With these principles and a little practice under your belt, you'll be hard-pressed to do a bad job, and you may well surprise yourself and further your career by turning in a superior performance!

♣ ♣ ♣

CHAPTER TWENTY

Conclusion:
Some Final Thoughts
on Private People

I n the course of reading this book, you've discovered and, I hope, practiced a number of speaking techniques, which have been presented in an order designed to help you move gradually from being a private to being a public person. You've come a long way, haven't you? From talking to yourself in the shower, to playing speaking games with your family, to telling inspirational and humorous stories before large groups, to defending your opinions in public debate.

It's almost time for me to give you your final send-off as you embark on other exciting adventures in platform speaking. But before I do, I can't resist a few final practical tips. The first, which I've already mentioned in another context, bears repeating, so here goes:

If you become serious about the business of making a good speech, I don't know of anything that could be of more help than a tape recorder. When you are beginning, you can say anything you want into it and then, in the privacy of your own room, listen to your recorded voice over and over again to hear how you *really* sound. Perhaps you've never known before that your voice has a faint nasal whine to it . . . or that you leave out the final *g* in all the words ending with "ing" . . . or that you are talking too fast to be easily understood . . . or that you are sucking in your breath after each sentence like an asthmatic pump . . . or that you slur your words almost unintelligibly whenever you get to the end of a thought.

Most people have never really heard their own voices. You ought to try it and play the tape over and over again no matter how painful you find it. I've often wished I could secretly tape-record some friend of mine at the dinner table or cocktail party to let him or her hear how sharp and sarcastic his voice becomes when talking about a mate. Hearing the sound of your own voice is a revelation; and without an expensive voice teacher or diction coach you can improve your own delivery by at least fifty percent through diligent and persevering effort to overcome the errors you hear yourself making.

With a tape recorder you can actually tape your own first speaking efforts. Get a friend to turn the machine on when you're introduced. Then, when you get back to the privacy of your own home, strap yourself firmly into a strong chair, swallow two aspirin, and listen to yourself . . . over and over . . . until you impress indelibly upon your brain the places where you were less than adequate.

Every good speaker I know regularly tapes his efforts and then does a thorough job of self-criticism.

Finally, get some tape cassettes of famous speakers who are doing "positive thinking" or "sales motivation" speeches and play them repeatedly, noting how they make transitions from topic to topic. You should especially watch how they vary their speed, intensity, and subject material. Cavett Robert, Zig Ziglar, Earl Nightingale, Ty Roberts, Dr. Denis Waitley, Ira Hayes, Dr. Norman Vincent Peale, David Cooper, and Og Mandino are but a few of the names that come to mind.

For my second tip, I would unhesitatingly recommend that you join a Toastmasters Club in your area. Here is where a group of friendly, supportive people can get together to give one another constructive criticism on a regular basis. You'll make new friends, improve your speaking dramatically, and learn a lot about a wide variety of subjects you'd never even thought of before.

The third tip is really a series of warnings:

- Don't try to be funny, flashy, or so original that you turn off your listeners. It is never smart to try something that is not natural or that is not tried and true. The old, well-known material that comes from your own life experience almost always does the job best.
- Pick the stories that illustrate the points you want to make and put it all together in an easy-flowing pattern with no sudden transitions.
- Be sure you have a logical beginning, a high point somewhere in the middle, and a sincere, prompt ending. And when in doubt . . . keep it short.
- When you say "and in conclusion" be sure that you ARE going to conclude. No matter what brilliant

thought comes to mind ... no matter how fascinating a story pops into your head ... once you've said "and finally" ... GET OFF!

All this advice I've been giving you will only amount to superficial technique unless you realize how fundamental good public speaking is to your own personal development. I'm not saying that you have to be a good speaker to be a good person. Far from it! Some of the nicest, most interesting people I know consistently refuse to expose themselves to an audience larger than two.

But I am saying this: I believe you have something important to say, and I don't think it's possible for you to have the impact on others you should and could have unless you learn how to communicate to groups as well as to individuals. There are times in your life when you are sitting on some important information or a thought that nobody else has expressed. If you share that idea, you'll enhance your relationship with other people and, at the same time, perhaps make the world a little better place—all because of the information or viewpoint you've passed on. But if you choose to remain silent—whether through fear or laziness—you'll detract to one degree or another from those qualities of reasoning, moral insight, and shared communication that distinguish each of us as human beings.

I believe that the reason that most people are afraid to speak publicly is that they're too self-centered. We each tend to constantly evaluate ourselves in light of what others think of us. We tend to be "other" directed. And because our personal flaws are more exposed when we're speaking to fifty people than when speaking to one, we tend to become fifty times more worried about the image we're projecting.

240

The real secret of overcoming this self-centeredness and opening yourself up to a public and not just a highly restrictive private communication is to focus on the other person, or on other people if you happen to be speaking to a group. Ask yourself, "How can I get my point across to the greatest number of people out there? What signals are they giving me that indicate I should change the pace or substance of my talk? What do I have to do to convince them that what I'm saying is really important to them?"

Before getting up to speak, get away for a few minutes to be by yourself to visualize the audience as a warm, friendly, responsive group. I occasionally excuse myself at a banquet to go to the men's room. What I actually do is to stand alone in a booth, close my eyes, and picture my listeners as curious, supportive friends who want me to succeed and who are waiting to get something from me that they can take with them to enhance or enrich their own lives. They are there to give me one of the most valuable gifts known to mankind: their time. I reassure myself that I have something to say that will repay them for this confidence.

So focus on getting outside yourself when you face your listeners. Keep your eyes and your attention always moving outward, rather than inward. Get more interested and absorbed in your audience than in yourself. And soon you'll find yourself moving with the ebb and flow of emotions and reactions being emitted by your listeners. When you begin to sense this spiritual and emotional movement in your audience, you'll find yourself being catapulted into a new dimension of communication with other people. And you'll begin to think, perhaps when you're in the middle of an address, "This is exhilarating! This is fun! Why haven't I been doing this all my life?"

So even if public speaking is number one among the *Book of Lists'* greatest human fears, it shouldn't be. For one thing, being able to talk well before people is a highly useful skill. And an ability to address large groups effectively is a key part of that total communication that can make us better human beings. But perhaps the most important thing to learn and remember in your attempt to banish your fright is that talking to groups can be fun. Believe me: After you've tried it a while, public speaking is the greatest pastime of all for private people!

Index